Pacific Rim
FLY FISHING:
The Unrepentant Predator

Jim Repine

Frank Amato

PORTLAND

DEDICATION:

"To my wife Sonia"

Published in 1995 by Frank Amato Publications, Inc.
PO Box 82112, Portland, Oregon 97282
(503) 653-8108

Softbound ISBN: 1-57188-025-9
UPC: 0-66066-00213-6

All photographs taken by the author except where noted.

Front and Back Cover photographs: Jim Repine
Frontispiece artwork: Colored charcoal pencil drawing by Sonia Repine.
Water color paintings on pages 2, 3 and pages 62, 63: Adolfo Nieto.
Book Design: Tony Amato

Printed in HONG KONG

1 3 5 7 9 10 8 6 4 2

CONTENTS

1

ORIGINS

*T*abby appeared frozen in a stalking position, ears up, eyes in a death-like stare, only an occasional twitch in her tail revealing the high tension within. The mouse had peered from its hole twice, disappearing after each time. Now it came out and started across the kitchen floor. The lightning was terrible swift.

Japanese shrine.

It hadn't rained for three days, a long dry spell at this altitude in high Honshu mountains, even in mid summer. Everything would parch by late morning. Yet now, as first sunlight filtered through thick, jungle-like foliage, lazy swirls of mist lightly moistened all they touched. Small gravel bars exposed here and there along the stream remained damp. It was that daily moment of transition from darkness to light when to say a drop of water, sparkling on a rose red wildflower petal was dew or mist, would have been impossible.

A small man in straw clothing, inverted conical hat, thatched shirt, thatched knee pants and woven sandals made his way down a trail beside the water. He noted things less practiced senses might not. The pungent scent of a passing black bear for example hanging thickly in a small clearing. There was movement in the brush. He stopped, attention complete. The 'movement' whistled. The he knew. It was harmless, a small tusked deer only.

Myriad birds sang in an even grander cacophony of insect sounds though not one unknown to the man. He ingested sounds, sights, smells, even the wet taste of mist with the comfort of familiarity. He was home, alert though at ease, an integral part of his environment. A long hand-carried bamboo pole with line attached signified his early morning intentions. The woven basket strapped over his shoulder explained further, why. He was going fishing—for something to eat.

A little farther the stream widened into a long pool dammed by two grand boulders. Its clarity was deceiving. Twelve feet to its deepest point appeared less than three or four, large rocks on the bottom a fraction of their actual size, and a half dozen Iwanas (char) grouped in an eddy monitoring the main stream flow could have been taken for seven or eight inchers.

A mayfly hatch was already emerging, not prolific though steady. The delicately formed creatures, light transparent green, were a tiny number eighteen hook size. They floated high on the surface, moving effortlessly with the current. And every now and again a fish for reasons apparent only to itself, would become attentive to a particular one. As the insect, now a tantalizing morsel, neared, the char's body quivered ever so slightly. A careful observer would have discerned a wee twitch in its tail. Signs of the same inner stirring felt by all predators at like moments.

Japanese gate.

Stream flow, distance and timing well computed the 'seven incher' grew to a sleek fourteen inch fish as it rose from depth to surface. It intercepted the fly, quietly sipped it in a smooth roll over, and dropped back among the others. The only evidence that the insect ever existed was a widening circle moving toward where the stream poured over the dam.

The angler arriving at the head of the pool stood for

awhile. He watched. He saw a rise and its spreading ring. Then another. He studied the water more closely, identifying the mayflies. Perhaps this same observation at this same pool in some previous period first inspired the creation of the tackle and methods he now employed? Perhaps not? Yet his cast was unerring, his imitation floating the feeding zone as the naturals had. Even the rolling take was alike, only this time a surprised char struggled for its life against bent bamboo. A short fight later and the ill fated creature gasped its last in the darkness of the creel.

This scene from the beginning of the 15th century could have been earlier. How much so no one knows. But that may not be the most fascinating part. What could surprise anglers more today is to learn that this early ancestor was using a tapered, horsehair line and dry flies fashioned over metal hooks. And that he was not only a fly fisherman but a purist, 'dry fly only' fly fisherman. Nor was he alone!

Japan's high mountain villages were for centuries sub-cultures of the rest of the population. Separated by elevation and dense vegetation, customs and traditions that never found their way to the rolling hills or wide fertile plains where most people lived, developed and flourished. It's understandable. Yet this lack of contact only deepens the mystery of how five hundred years ago and beyond, fly fishing so similar to European angling of the same period was discovered and practiced in Japan's mountain cultures. And why was this knowledge confined to such an isolated portion, the highlands, of one of the least known countries of the time?

In England where American anglers more often look for origins of our peculiar approach to fishing, Dame Julianna Berner's famous *Treatise of Fishing With An Angle*, whoever wrote it, verifies that basics as far as tackle was concerned were happening at the same time there. Though less clear, early Egyptian hieroglyphic evidence shows not only that people took fish with feathered lures but the angler's clothing is upper

Mountain Stream.
FACING PAGE: Wes Jordan rod with ancient style Japanese creel.

class. In other words, it was sport, a diversion of pleasure even then rather than solely food gathering.

A century and a half after the *Treatise of Fishing With An Angle,* in *The Compleat Angler,* Isaac Walton's piscator converting an at first derisive venador (hunter) to higher, more contemplative joys of angling, is obviously a gentleman of leisure. They stay in favored inns, sleep "twixt" scented sheets, eat and drink the best foods, wines and ales with ample time for fun. Yet little less emphasis is on table preparation than on catching the fish. It was bait and fly fishing in a delightful pastiche of high level sport, music, poetry and fine dining.

Only in the short second portion of this most famous of all angling books, Charles Cotton writes exclusively of angling with a fly. However Thomas Barker's book, authored before Walton's, offered specific instructions for tying flies streamside to better imitate what natural fish were taking at the moment. Matching the hatch.

Nor is it conceivable there weren't other places with similar manifestations in centuries past. Travel between England and France, with the Spanish World not much more difficult, make it improbable that information so fascinating wouldn't make the rounds. But what started where? Who told who? There are doubtless surprises to come.

It was a warm September afternoon in eastern Virginia, Lakeside, Virginia to be precise. Named for a large pond in this now Richmond suburb, in 1944 it was still a small rural community. World War Two's cruel bloodshed had been roaming the planet since Hitler's push into Sudatenland. My brother was in the South Pacific flying fighter plane missions off an aircraft carrier, a hero grander and more believed in by me at ten years old than God. But his stature was assured in my eyes before all that. He was the first one to take me fishing.

I was at the creek just below the namesake lake. Worms were my game in those days, fished at the end of a green cord line attached to a cane pole, red, white and green striped bobber floating my squirming bait just off the bottom. I remember it as clearly as kissing Eula Zimmerman on the mouth a few years later. It's hard to say which of those events had the deeper impact.

Ching and I came to the creek right after lunch, our daily custom all summer. Though school, that most tedious curse to boys who prefer to fish, had started on Monday, bringing our bucolic weekday afternoons to naught, this was Saturday. We hurried. My skinny legs were a twenty minute circular blur as the bike, fishing pole across the handle bars, sped through the neighborhood. Ching's four shorter legs moved as quickly as he panted along beside me.

The worms had come from our front lawn the night before. They were long, strong nightcrawlers, had for only sprinkling a portion of yard, waiting a few minutes, then returning with a flashlight to pick them up. I carried them in a tin can, the open lid curled over one handlebar grip. The trick, my brother let me in on, was to hook them so fish couldn't see the point, bream then apparently more clever than now. So skewered they wiggle with allure underwater, promotion to all critters with fins to, "Eat Here."

It took another fifty years for my sensibilities to develop enough to write in, *How To Fly Fish Alaska,* Frank Amato Publications, the following:

"What I despise though is callous, cruel disrespect displayed toward a fellow creature. Sometime, if you have never done this, hold a fish in your hands that you have landed. Be very gentle. Keep it in the water and consider every aspect of this wondrous being. Examine the design. Let yourself be fascinated with the marvel of its coloration.

The rock on the small stream in Virginia where I first saw a fish rise to a fly.

Prowling brown trout.

Ponder over its lifestyle. Think of all the rejuvenating, soul mending adventures fish offer. But mostly, absorb the sensuously pulsing energy of its life force, let your own flow back in answer, and never again believe that taking another's life is of little consequence."

I admit bias among critters though, like giving extreme consideration to trout while favoring the extinction of mosquitoes. A bug, any bug (favored trout tidbit or not) crawling in or on my pajamas after I settle into bed with night light and book, is doomed to instant, violent death. This has cost me expensive lamp shades, light bulbs, dented book covers and explosive reactions from an otherwise gentle wife. But comfortingly, one rarely encounters earthworms among the covers.

Anyway on this memorable day what happened meant, among other things, a radical departure from low, course methods, a first step up from meat to sport. As we sat on a streamside boulder, hapless worm hidden in the depths below us, huge beech trees blended shade in elixic proportion to fall breezes. We were almost dozing when it happened.

Something I now call a 'hatch' was going on. Mayflies? It was too far back to be exact but these loveliest of insects hold another of my preferred positions, dreamy recollection including only favored players. Floating on a gentle current feeding my worm pool came an insect, diaphanous wings like sails, antennae and tails in the air at opposite ends. We were spellbound with precognition. I recall the excitement.

As ominous as a surfacing U-boat, from the depths of my black pool rose the largest, darkest old bream in Lakeside Creek. He came up slowly, positioned and timed precisely to meet and eat the fly. I remember no sound. The insect and fish vanished. And with them my worm days.

Some philosopher or other said that if there were no God humanity should create one. It seems also that if there were no fly fishing some Japanese mountain dweller, English gentleman of leisure or maybe a French farmer, Spanish duke, a New York City dentist or some small boy and his dog surely someone somewhere would see a trout rise and grasp its implications. Perhaps they and others did that. I can only say that again despite my inability to define the magic of something so pervasively enchanting, for a half century of immeasurable pleasure, I owe deep gratitude to someone or something I cannot see.

> "So if this antiquity of Angling, which for my part I have not forced, shall, like an ancient family, be either an honor or an ornament to this virtuous art which I profess to love and practice, I shall be the gladder that I made an accidental mention of it."
> —Izaak Walton, 1653.

ORIGINS

2

KILL OR RELEASE

*T*he young salesman handed the form to Mr. Katzman. If he signed, it would mean the largest order in company history. His preparation and presentation had been his best ever, he knew it. Katzman raised his pen—then hesitated, slowly rereading everything. He shook his head, looking doubtful.

"I'll need this stuff in 10 days, no later!" he smiled and quickly scrawled his name.

I am a predator. I suspect you are one too. I have been aware of it from my earliest recollections though it's only in recent years that I feel the need to identify or understand the trait. My motives have been mixed however with an opposing side. Trophy collector or zoo keeper, Orion the Hunter or Saint Francis, I have ambled through my space and time bouncing from one persuasion to the other, often intermingling the two.

I almost always have had a dog for example, at times several, and without exception loved them. In early youth my cruelties to these best friends were innocent, forgetting to feed them promptly, teasing them to entertain pals, lesser friends than my victims, that sort of thing. And all of the wild creatures, snakes, turtles, frogs, etc. that I incarcerated in shoe boxes, chicken wire pens and home made cages were so treated in misguided optimism that we would somehow grow to love each other, pet and trusted master. Yet never discovering a frog or turtle that would wag its tail or lick my hand, compassion each time overcame selfishness and I found satisfaction in setting my inmates free. Still other critters fared less happily for my presence.

With the exception of immediate family and a handful of friends I have never found deeper fascination and love for a fellow creature than I felt for the various blueticks and beagles I shared home and field with. A professional musician from my fourteenth year to the thirty first, nothing from Mozart to Willie Nelson stirred me more profoundly than baying hounds. Considering however that these man/dog bondings were founded in day and night torment of rabbits and raccoons, 'animal lover' scarcely described me, my sentiments more akin to the dogs I loved.

My meat gathering instincts were triggered by my mom. She grew up on an Illinois mule farm in a family of older brothers. They all hunted and fished. It was diversion from long hard hours of work yet serious business, putting food on the table. Her sporting tales so kindled my imagination that when we 'moved to the country', leaving a city suburb for a newly developed one in an adjoining county where you could at least see farm land in the distance, I began my hunting and fishing career. Thumb size crawfish living in holes along the open drainage ditch in front of our house where my first prey species. I was five years old.

I say hunting and fishing because it was a mix. My equipment was a short pole, string attached, with a bent pin hook at the terminal end baited with bread. And I was attempting to capture something with fish at the end of its name. But my quarry in this circumstance was a land based animal, not living in creek, river or lake. In any event I spent my fifth summer in sunsuit and barefoot trying to lure a crawfish out of its hole and into my mom's frying pan. Though I got several up and almost out of their sanctuaries, they always managed to wiggle free in time to scurry back down into dark safety. But a lifetime predator was born.

Next came heady days learning to worm and bobber fish with my brother Bob which included a stringer, killing and cleaning, mom's magic skillet and crispy, delicious things to eat. Then the 'mayfly awakening', a Sears and Roebuck level wind outfit, a loving gift from a non fishing father who would rather have had me take up violin, plugging for bass and pickerel; all eventually leading to the big time. Hunting.

For that milestone my mentor was a much admired older boy living three houses up the block. This hunter almost reached my bother's height for sharing an afternoon with a kid. He went off to war not long after. When people told of his enlistment they used a different tone than for other youngsters off to the Army or Navy. In open awe, they said:

"Boo Quarles joined the Marines!"

Though I had no idea then of the difference, I knew that if a young man could hide from a wild animal, patience unending, never moving an eyebrow until it was lulled from alertness, to then kill it with one clean shot, he would be a formidable foe to our country's enemies. Marines must be very special, I thought. I watched him take five plump gray squirrels on that wondrous afternoon. And then an unforeseen thing happened. I was struck dumb. He gave me a turn.

Sitting under a huge hickory tree with nut cuttings (pieces of shell dropped by feeding squirrels) all around me I kept mentally repeating my instructor's sparse words:

"Stay here, don't move. Listen for the squirrel coming through the trees. Don't take the safety off until you are ready to shoot, aim careful and pull the trigger real smooth—don't jerk it!"

I doubted my patience. I was cramped and my nose itched as an early evening mosquito landed on the back of my hand. Sight and feel of the tortuous insect possessed me. Outrage at the advantage it was taking was worse than its stinging blood probe. Temptation to smash it was rising. Then I heard something.

A faint rustle, far away. I came alert, straining to hear more. A distant breeze? Long minutes passed, cramps and madly itching mosquito bite regaining my attention. It came again, closer, more distinct. Something was out there in the trees and making its way toward me. Excitement dispelled miseries.

It's a unique emotion, predator expectation. To call it pleasing is inexact, stirring perhaps. In intense manifestation it's pulse rushing exhilaration and chilling fear, elation of expectation and anxiety of failure or unanticipated consequences. Though the same, it comes in degrees. Watching a bobber disappear from the surface of a bream pond doesn't trigger

Hatchi, the author's dog.
FACING PAGE: Virginia swamp country.

the same height of sensation as shooting an arrow into an angry grizzly, but no matter the level, for me, the thrill is always there.

My squirrel was taking forever, stopping in each hickory along the way to check things out. Yet if eternity was what it took, I wouldn't move. I would wait for my moment, especially knowing that not far away Boo Quarles was watching. Blood pounded. What if I missed? The thought rattled me. A throat gripping shiver went to my heart. Suddenly a limb halfway up the tree bent noisily down as the unsuspecting critter landed from an adjoining oak and made its way toward the trunk. I raised the .22. The squirrel froze. But fortune of fortunes, in full view.

At the instant of the shot, a leaf an inch above the intended victim's head came free and spiraled slowly down. My game disappeared around the limb, and my coach's voice spoke from a short distance to my left:

"Not bad! You almost got him."

Virginia gray squirrel.

Because my mom cooked anything I brought home as long as I prepared it for the pan, we ate many bream, bass, pickerel, catfish, squirrels and rabbits over the next several years and I still appreciate the environmental kindredship of taking subsistence from its bounty. Then in my teens came hounds.

This time my family did move to the country buying a small farm with a pleasant old house. There was a barn, outbuildings and an eighty tree apple orchard. I was sixteen, had a baby blue, '40 Ford convertible and was playing bass fiddle around Richmond in a combo. Quite a sport for those times! But a new love took over my life.

There had already been Juanita Lacy, Anne Voorhees, Peggy Bragg, and Eula Zimmerman with Patsy Hicks and Mary Alice Fobian soon to come, yet as lovely as all of these young ladies were (and hopefully still are), like I said, nothing ever enchanted me more than baying hounds. I met Bobby Magee at my new high school, I immediately liked him and was enthralled with his tales about something called night hunting. His family had moved to Virginia from North Carolina, his drawl slightly different as he lit a new coal in my predatory soul:

"You do it at night with dogs and carbide lanterns. Not just any dogs, you need hounds, ones that will only run 'coons cause if they 'trash' they might take off after a fox and you'll run all night for nothing. Or worse if they take to chasing deer you might not find them again for days—or never! There's nothing prettier though than big hounds running the woods at night. It's kind of mysterious sounding though you know what a good dog is doing from the way he bays. Sometimes it's pitch dark and once the dogs get a track going you got to follow, no matter what! Swamps, creeks or briar patches, they don't mean nothing when your 'coon hunting."

He stopped, sensing the effect:

"You want to try it sometime?" He smiled.

"Can we go tonight?" I smiled back.

I remember a night a few years later, the hot convertible long since swapped for an old International Scout. Not a great date auto, it was an ideal rig for three or four blueticks and two or three hunters. It reeked of wet dogs and carbide with touches of skunk lingering after a midnight encounter our, not always perfect, dogs had with a white striped critter. It was a savory collage of treasured incidents, a nasal sonnet of luscious experiences smelled rather than heard. Even now my wife struggles with my affection for dog smell.

It was early September, weather mild with warm breezes through a huge corn patch that we had parked beside. At the field's edge was a vast swamp of gnarled oaks draped with Spanish moss, mist swirling up off the water. There were delightful night sounds, frogs, birds, an occasional gray fox splashing after a frog, a snorting deer startled by a fat opossum scuttling through dry leaves at the edge of the water. And as always the million voice insect chorus of a southern swamp. The moon was three quarters full, passing in and out behind small clouds. I cannot dream of sweeter intoxicants.

Three hounds pummeled down off the Scout's tailgate, bumping shoulders like brawny football players emerging from a dressing room. Their infectious excitement dissolved into the moonlight. Bobby's face was alight from a match igniting the low hissing carbide gas. There was barely time for me to do the same as King our largest, most beautifully voiced dog let out a long, night rending bawl that would have teared the eyes of Pavarotti.

I have never come close to adequately describing what a hunting dog's bay evokes in me. It's not a conscious impression. It doesn't bring specific images to mind. It's emotional, something deep, a gut feeling, if you will pardon a trite expression. Once felt you won't wonder why ancient Greeks taught that the heart and not the brain was the fount of human response. For the attuned it's like the primal emotion elicited by a wolf howl.

The scent was fresh, the track hot. We had unwittingly chased the 'coon from the field with our arrival. All three dogs were in full cry, a wild racing sprint that could crowd the raccoon up the first sizeable tree it came to. Yet as we ran as fast as hip boots allow, everything stopped. No birds, frogs, insects, nothing! Only eerie silence.

In 'coon hunting this is often the time of truth. Either the quarry is up a tree and the dogs are trying to verify which one (checking it's called) or it has sneaked away through the water. Insects began singing again, hesitant at first. Birds and frogs followed. We heard our dogs then, well into the swamp. They were giving intermittent voice, nosing out a puzzle, a telltale scent crossing a small island, a whiff of spoor clinging over an exposed log, all the while the trail cooling as the clever old ringtail gained ground.

The chase became slower and slower until we decided to declare the 'coon the winner, call in the dogs and look for another track. But before I could raise horn to mouth all three dogs opened at the end of the swamp and we knew that our competitor had blundered. He left the confusing safety of the swamp. Raccoon still in front, hounds fast closing, they headed straight at us, throttles open full.

We saw the animal's eyes in our lantern glow as it saw us, swerved toward the swamp and skittered up the highest swamp oak in the area. We were jubilant. We had won! We? Well the dogs were ours, yes or no?

That's some of 'coon hunting and at least a glimpse of how it excited my urge to predate. And in the beginning I confess enjoying the kill, the experience somehow unfinished without it. But an important thing gained then was awakening to the absurdity of always carrying an animal instinct to its full conclusion. Why butcher the source of the pleasure? Wasn't it the raccoon after all that made the whole wonderful madness possible? What could be more stupid than eliminating another one every time we won? And though it would take another twenty years to come to fruition I learned sport fishing's great philosophical advance, catch and release, chasing raccoons through the beguiling swamps of eastern Virginia.

"And I am a lover of hounds; I have followed many a pack of dogs many a mile, and heard many merry huntsmen make sport and scoff at Anglers."

— Izaak Walton, 1653.

Swamp trees.

Old survivor.

3
TO FOOL A FISH

he big tom hadn't eaten in two weeks. In normal conditions taking meat from the small heard of skinny mule deer yarded in the meadow below him would be easy, but he was weak. The Bitterroot winter was the worst in half a century, week after week of deep snow and marrow freezing temperatures. A mistake now could be the old lion's end!

As furtive as my glances in their direction are when I accompany my wife through the endless malls she gets wind of and though a squad of L.A. riot cops would have a tough struggle dragging me inside one of them, from the quick glimpses I do manage, ladies' lingerie shops must be titillating places to browse. Yet even if avant customs someday offer men that unembarrassed opportunity, you will still find Sonia Repine more often fighting boredom as I fondle goodies displayed in fly fishing shops. And nothing there fascinates me more than flies.

The first time I tied a hackle feather on a hook as instructed by my *Introduction to Fly Tying* book and wound it behind the hook eye it was another of my great angling moments. As magic as doves flying from empty top hats, an insect blossomed in my hands. I was twelve. The next morning a small bream slurped it off the surface at the edge of some lily pads. High euphoria was mine! Still it wasn't just quick action or the tugging struggle following. There was extraordinary stimulation in the deception.

I loved practical jokes until one going awry caused me to quit them. Fooling a fish with something artificial, especially a fly I create and craft, sweetens my catch. And though I seldom do it, anglers who come to the water with vise and materials, adding 'on the spot hatch matching' to their repertories doubtless broaden their pleasure. So if duping a simple creature

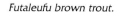

Futaleufu brown trout.

with a brain smaller than an English pea, less intelligent than a teenage boy (if you can believe that), isn't too bullying to be sport then that aspect of fly fishing is one of its grand marvels.

On the Futaleufu River in southern Chile where my wife and I have a farm, fall comes on the twenty first day of March and with it, give a few days on either side, appear a fair number of larger brown trout. The odd big brown is always there, still it's more often later in the season, snowcaps returned to higher peaks, when a day or two of serious angling produces something in the twenty five to thirty inch range. Serious means heavy shooting heads, long, sixty foot and better, casts, drifting deeper recesses of the runs, much patience and large, dark, weighted flies.

I don't pretend to know much about what fish do or why. I hope I never do. One can analyze angling so much and become so knowledgeable of all its aspects that the name for a creature as delightful as a mayfly becomes pretentiously elongated Greek, less appealing than chemical definitions on medicine bottles.

Fly shop book shelves groan under the ever compounding weight. Fly fishing isn't war to end war or man's final effort to banish pain and sorrow. It's of less moment. And while the 'egghead' approach for those with a bent for it can seem an enhancement, different from streamside fly tying, if you go too far down the path you can diminish another quality of a pleasant diversion in proportion to the distance traveled. The mystery, romance if you will, spontaneous creativity might even be a closer definition; whatever the magic is, it withers a bit with the death of each potential surprise. Sterile 'knowing' displacing pregnant fascination appears to me more loss than achievement. As a poor yet believing Christian, discovering now that God is right handed yet reels with his left or that angels carry leader chronometers could convert joyful hope to something grim enough to jeopardize my gate pass. Why would I want to lessen the very fuel of my enchantment? Still, balance is best and there are things one needs to grasp!

If you want to do battle with old Patagonian brutes for example you must learn to get down, way down, with something heavy, large and dark. If you want to improve your chances further, your fly needs movement, shimmying, living motion that brings to mind rabbit fur or marabou feathers. And then if you want to really maximize your odds, add sparkle and flash. In several seasons of fishing this water I have evolved from number eight Black Woolly Buggers through sixes and even fours. I added lead, replaced marabou with more durable rabbit fur and applied various tinsel, flash materials, etc. And the catch rate has increased.

Happily, I don't know why? It would be easy to formulate another of those ceaseless, all-knowing theories, yet the truth is that the success may be nothing more than cyclic gain in population or maybe the natural food supply is down, the trout hungrier. Or, hurrah, it could be something that no one has yet thought of. Please, if you know the answer, spare me. Let me relish the mystery for another season or two.

I must tell you that I don't want to catch a fish every cast. On the water more than a hundred days a year, a negative thing, one of few, I experienced in twenty five consecutive years of fishing Alaska was too many angling days with too many, too large and too easily caught fish. Everyone who enjoys our sport should have some days like that, yet too many too often make the catch too common. It can lose its charm. As remarkable a fishery as it is, Alaska almost did that to me.

Over the past fifty years I have observed and come to recognize a phenomenon that I believe is irrefutable. What accounts for those few anlgers who always catch more and bigger fish is their degree of predator instinct and to how fine an edge this instinct has been honed. Claudio Arrau, the recently deceased Chilean virtuoso, was born with unusual musical aptitude, a prodigy, yet his worldwide acclaim resulted from a lifetime spent, in practice and concert, playing the piano. He spent more than eighty years developing everything from technique to theory but it was constant exercise of an elevated instinct that carried his success beyond so many others. Lee Wulff is my best case in anglers.

Chilean garden flowers.
FACING PAGE: Joan Wulff casting,
Futaleufu River.

Apple blossoms in the Espolon Valley
near Futaleufu.
PAGES 16 & 17: Futaleufu village Chile.

On an unnamed coastal river in Alaska so remote, even with two hundred thousand visiting anglers annually crowding most other water, you can still fish in solitude, I spent one of several days with Lee and his wife Joan. There were three or four others in the party, a guide and what looked like a thousand bright, sea run silver salmon. This river isn't wide, in many portions no farther than sixty feet to the opposite bank. Each clear pool was jammed with sea bright fish and the guide had effective patterns to give out. Every fourth or fifth cast produced a jolting strike with an accompanying slam, bang, high jumping, sizzling run, fight. It was one of those days—except for Lee Wulff.

Lee Wulff and Jim Repine.

It was different for him. He didn't cast farther or with a tighter loop than the others. As hard as I studied his methods there were no unique movements, teasing twitches or the like in his retrieve. Ever an experimenter, he changed patterns once or twice but I quickly followed with identical flies. The only explanation for why he hooked up on more of his casts than not had to be an acute predator sense, and the eighty years at the time he had been sharpening it. As if he could see into their minds, time after time, he placed his fly in front of the one salmon in the pod that was at that moment ready to take. If you don't have this gift, in some measure at least, don't be discouraged, fly angling without it won't hold you captive long enough to forget how to bowl or play racquet ball.

I don't remember his name if I ever heard it but I shared time with another man who appeared to be in his eighties, though with guys like that it's hard to tell. He was wrinkled, a bit stooped and faltering of step when a guide helped him from the float plane. Yet his snow white hair was thick, his eyes clear and what little he said that night was spoken in a steady, resonant voice.

"I've never taken a really large fish, nothing over about six pounds. In Pennsylvania where I fish, two and three pounders are trophies. But I've done it all my life and now I want to add to it, catch something really big maybe just once. I want to know what it feels like." The slow burning logs in the huge stone fireplace reflected from his glass as we toasted his quest.

"Fish are here! Egg fishermen killed a thirty four pound one this afternoon and they nailed one yesterday that was over fifty. You have a real shot at it." I said with confidence as we headed for the tying bench and together created something big, black, heavy and as flashy as a carnival kewpie doll.

There was no question the elements were falling in place for the old guy. His arrival on the Talachulitna River in southcentral Alaska was a few days after the king salmon run began, in time for holding fish to have increased to good numbers. The weather was mixed, sunshine, misting rain, no bad winds and a water level just low enough to corral salmon in resting places without impeding their entrance into the river. All he needed was luck for another twenty four hours.

"I only have one day, tomorrow! A trip like this is a bunch of bucks for an old codger like me. A day here with a guide was all I could do but when you get old enough to realize your clock isn't going to tick forever, well. . ." If he finished the thought, it was lost in the crackle of the fire.

Before sleeping I looked around the log cabin where I was spending the week. I had lived in this far north wonder world for ten years then, spent hundreds of other nights in similar Jack London settings, listening to night sounds, wandering porcupines, fox, startled moose, even hungry grizzlies and smelled the rain-freshened spruce forest. For an old Virginia crawfish

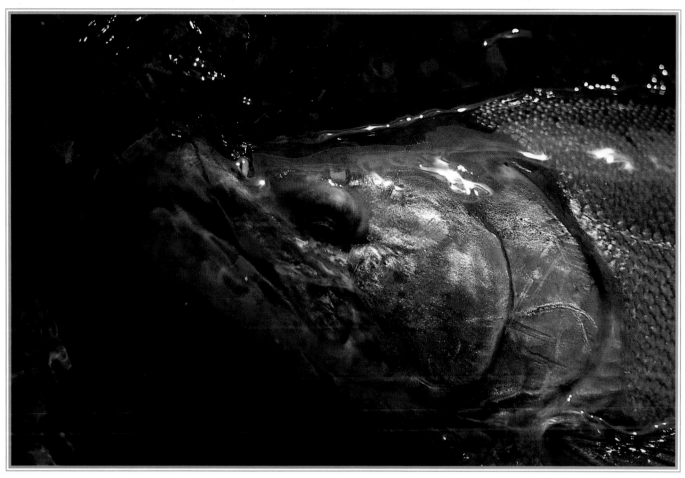

Silver salmon.

hunter who never grew up it was dreamy stuff, awake or sleeping. A restless salmon boiled the river's surface. I wondered if my new friend heard it? How long had he fantasized and saved for just one night and day of this? Alaska remains for me a never ending sequence of marvels, yet how would I value one day of its fishing if I knew it was the only one in my life?

My next day's gear was two camera bodies and enough lenses, tripods, etc., to make an otherwise even tempered burro buck. Thanks to mild, ever changing weather with varying light conditions, photo opportunities were endless. As in all Talachulitna Septembers when sun backlights rain misted leaves in high cottonwoods, they glowed like hand buffed gold. Against a patch of rich blue sky they were dazzling. At times cone shaped radiance poured down through cloud breaks causing moose meadows to gleam with an illusory effect that would have made miracles seem normal. Fish were moving up rapids to resting water before finishing their few final miles to spawn. The river was crystalline and more than once hiking beside it toward the pool where I planned to hold morning court, there were aggressive swirls from restless monster salmon.

In this situation male and female, though having stopped feeding at their entry into freshwater will often take a fly. Presentation is the important factor, the fish seldom mouthing anything that's more than inches off the bottom. They will sometimes move a few feet to the side to grab yet almost never come up to do it. If they were giant trout their rolling and swirling could signify feeding. Japanese friends of mine and I once found large sheefish far north from there doing that, streamers simulating minnows igniting wild action. So with no interest in food why do these fish strike? Theories aside, no one knows.

A long lens attached to the camera on the tripod, a wide angle on another to be hand held and a folding stool prepared me for the day. Muffled sounds from a jet boat starting up at the lodge floated up over the clamoring rapids below the pool. I wondered who that first angler of the morning was and whether he and his guide would head down to the nearby mouth or slip over the rushing water below me and into my pool. The powerful motor soon roared out of hearing downriver. Then a second boat followed.

I began to fear that everyone would go the same way leaving me nothing to photograph.

To Fool a Fish

At last though a motor started, idled for a few moments and started upriver. The first shot I took on that fateful dawn was of an eighteen foot, bright aluminum jet boat emerging from swirling mist like an apparition. Its flashing silver bow with huge red Coast Guard numbers gleaming blood scarlet, plunged through a shaft of sunlight. The guide, standing aft, tiller in one hand, throttle in the other, slowed to a cautious crawl. I recognized his client. It was the elder angler. Great, I thought.

The man refused to hurry. He had come to the boat rigged and I thought I saw that he was using the fly we had tied. As he listened to his guide's instructions he continued to sit, watching, I believe savoring, everything around him. When he spotted me on my little rock beach, he gave a cheery wave.

Then his reveries were shattered by another unexplained salmon spectacle. A mammoth bull king crashed up through the calm surface, cleared the water and splashed back down with enough commotion to cause a beaver crossing the river to give the water a resounding smack with its tail and dive. Two large mallard drakes flapped up in alarm. Not even my imperturbable friend could stand all that. By the time quiet returned, I was framing his first cast.

A lifelong, small stream trouter, the nine weight graphite borrowed for the trip wasn't part of his accustomed gear. But he had practiced enough before coming to get a consistent fifty foot line out. His guide's choice of the pool was probably based on this as the area of the river mouth requires longer casts. Still there was a flair to his efforts, a fluidity and economy of movement speaking of long years on those streams. He was soon doing everything, especially presentation, with skill enough. I am sure this man caught his share of Pennsylvania's stream trout. But enticing a king salmon to bite can be a long tiring exercise.

After three or four hours the big rod, big line, big fly combination became cruel penance. With increasing incident the caster lost control. At first it was slight, the line lacking speed not moving as far as needed or a fault in accuracy, until there came a steady decrease in casts. At noon we lunched together.

Ham sandwiches, potato chips and beer were never tastier as the last clouds of the day passed over. Yet neither cool fall breezes or warm sunshine dispelled our growing apprehension. As far as we knew the morning hadn't produced even an interested glance from a salmon. Still, though less frequent during the bright light of midday, an occasional fish swirl taunted us with proof of their continued presence. As much as I tout the unexpected, angling irony can play hard with the most deserving.

Contrary to human wisdom fishless days are good things, heightening elation when success

Kenai dawn.

does come but when there is only one shot at a lifetime dream it's different. The guide and I hoped hard for our companion's afternoon as they got back into the boat and moved to a different position in the pool. Still by five o'clock the only thing we shared was deepening gloom.

One of the angling's best teachings however is that skill and perseverance applied long enough overcome poor luck. The old man broke his jinx just before six by deftly setting a hook in the jaw of the first salmon he ever felt. The fish went nuts! It ran, lunged and jumped all over the pool before tiring enough to be netted. But it was small, maybe fifteen pounds. True it was the largest fish this angler had ever landed or hooked yet not the Alaskan behemoth he had hoped for.

"I am satisfied!" He yelled across to me. "But there's another half an hour to go. I am not going to quit."

His blood had heated. It was apparent in his cast, crisp and controlled like his early morning efforts. And the third drift made it happen. The line stopped, he lifted the rod, felt solid weight and struck. Nothing moved. He struck again, this time with more force then he had ever before applied. It set off a massive detonation. A huge bulge of water swelled up and exploded in all directions as an enraged 'salmon grande' leaped high into red evening sunlight. The scene is forever etched in my mind though unrecorded by forgotten cameras.

The battle was long and exhaustive for angler, guide and fish. The salmon did everything that fifty pound, sea energized fish can. Yet in the end inflamed angler wilted into sad desperation as he sensed life's ultimate fulfillment now so close, being taken from him. The unwilling player prolonged doom for a long, long hour. Then slowly, ever so slowly, he allowed himself to be led into the guide's waiting net. I could only make out silhouettes in the failing light.

A straining net with hapless fish lifted over the boat's side was obvious, congratulatory gestures and sounds between guide and guided, the same. But what happened next wasn't explained until later.

The fine elder predator, a small stream trout fisherman starring in his own grandest production, leaned over the fish for a better view. He slipped and fell into the net, arms clutching his prey. Whether from mortal ecstasy or heart failure, he was as dead as the proverbial mackerel. Sad tale or fateful triumph? It depends on your own predator perspective!

"But he that hopes to be a good Angler must not only bring an inquiring, searching, observing wit, but he must bring a large measure of hope and patience, and a love and propensity to the art itself; but once having got and practiced it, then doubt not but Angling will prove to be so pleasant, that it will be like virtue, a reward to itself."
—Izaak Walton, 1653.

4

THE GREATLAND

*T*he bear, a dark brown six year old tundra grizzly, weighed at least six hundred pounds. When he walked waves rippled through his rich, silver tipped pelt, undulating like breezes stir wheat fields. But now he crouched, inching through low brush like a stalking bengal, the unsuspecting young cow moose still twenty yards away. A twig snapped! She bolted—too late?

I crossed the Alaska border on August 19, 1968. No good with dates, I recall few birthdays, anniversaries, my Marine Corps discharge date or many others but this unforgettable day never leaves me.

After an adventurous eight weeks crossing North America from Chester, Virginia to Tok Junction, Alaska we were authentic pioneers. Our prairie schooner was a Chevrolet pickup with a camper shell, trailing an eighteen foot, cabined john boat. The camper space we used for that, the boat and trailer our burdened beasts loaded to groaning with everything from household goods and fishing gear to clothing and our five year old, Virginia-reared, Siberian husky, Eski. Looking like the pilgrims we were, we crossed the border at dusk and pulled into a campground.

Though exhausted from the long day's drive, I had trouble falling asleep that night. A wife, eight year old daughter and I had made our "Alaska or Bust" brag happen. The part that seemed the greater challenge, the trip to this point was finished. Yet it was then when my confidence wavered. Who had made it to the last frontier? A young dolt and his trusting followers neither of whom knew anything of what lay ahead. The rest of my night was fitful.

Then as dawn struggled with final dark shadows the campground broke into frantic activity. First came voices, men's pre coffee voices, gruff, sleep slurred but strong, commanding. Vehicles all around us coughed and roared into life. A staging area for an armed assault? The sounds said so. 'An anxiety related dream?' I wondered as I half dressed and stepped from the camper shell.

It was all there, weapon laden men in camouflage, idling combat vehicles fuming and quivering, lusting for hot gulps of petrol. But this wasn't the Marine Corps! I had been in that. With no two uniforms alike and every vehicle of dissimilar modification, this was latter day Pancho Villa with Army/Navy store outfitting and home made tundra buggies. The local militia? An Eskimo uprising? Now I really wasn't sure what I had led my little family to, as Eski stood in the boat barking at everything.

"Excuse me! Er, ah, excuse me but what's happening? There's some kind of trouble?" I approached a man with a huge rifle in his hand, a scimitar size bowie knife on his belt and a .44 magnum revolver in a shoulder holster.

"It's August 20th!" He said it like I was Scrooge asking what day it was—on Christmas morning.

"Yeah?" My expression was blank.

"Where the hell are you from man?" Not rancored, he was puzzled. Then eyeing our Virginia license plate with the "Alaska or Bust" bumper sticker beside it he smiled. "It's the opening day of moose season! Welcome to Alaska!"

Why had I come? What would inspire a young man with family to leave the comfortable environs of his rearing, security of caring relatives, friends, job connections, etc., to resettle in a place he had only read about? The reasons thousands do it all over the world each year vary with each person but in hindsight I understand mine.

The Coopers, Gary and James Fenimore, Walt Disney, Jack London, Donald Culross Peattie, Hemingway and Ruark; all fanned my predator juices at the same time my boyhood haunts were falling daily to relentless pre mall, pre housing development, bulldozers. My buffalo herds, charging rhinos, proud Sioux warriors and wild goose flocks that blackened the sun, dreams I could indulge only in the woods, were crashing around me. When the urge to flee began I'm not sure but the precise moment of decision remains clear.

Alaska moose.
FACING PAGE: Alaska brown bear.
PAGES 24 & 25: Trophy Alaskan rainbow.

We lived near the Blackwater Swamp in southeast Virginia and had a boat, the same one we hauled to Alaska. It was aluminum, a slight vee in the bow yet flat bottomed with a very shallow draft. I wasn't aware then of jet units so a 35 horsepower short shaft motor and a fourteen foot pole put us about anywhere we dreamed to be. It was a late summer weekend and I spent hours steering and poling us into the most remote portion of a vast (for there) wild place. We butter fried a half dozen crispy bream taken soon after arriving, enjoyed them with potato salad and bread, and talked until darkness brought mosquitoes in repellent-defying numbers. Snuggled into light, soft padded sleeping bags behind bug proof netting, we soon slumbered in peace. Great stuff!

Sometime after midnight though what one doctor diagnosed as a lazy bladder urged me on deck. The moon was full, creating silvery reflections and silhouettes of water, moss draped cypress and misty surroundings, eerie yet wonderful. I had done it! We were camped in wild environs, for once out of the greed debauchery. I understood then why wolves sometimes howl for nothing more than joy. My rapture wasn't to last.

I heard a large truck to my left a long way off but coming closer. To my horror the noise

Alaska salmon brooks falls.

Alaska black bear.

grew louder and louder until at its closest point there was an angry airhorn blast followed by a thud. Some poor deer was too slow on the highway. I felt helpless agony at its bleating as it died beside the pavement. Afterward there were dogs barking from three houses in different directions. I knew the longer I hesitated the slimmer my chances of ever knowing real wilderness would be.

In less than two months I listened to Horace Greely, quit my job, sold everything ten years of marriage had accumulated, including three beloved coonhounds and arrived as far west and north as the United States extends. Looking at the mad scene around me on that first morning though, it was difficult not to wonder if we had come far enough.

Those first several months were incredible, getting settled in a modest Anchorage apartment that cost four times per month what our log house with a large yard and garage rented for in Chester, Virginia. Realizing that $800 socked away, cash I had sold my dogs for, not only burned my soul as Judas money but wouldn't pay two months rent was a jolt. Food gathering would no longer just be sport.

At Sears Roebuck where I took a job selling televisions it was soon apparent that nine tenths of the male employees and a generous number of the ladies only worked there to support their fishing and hunting. It was the primary subject of all discussions, break times, between customers, often with customers and too often while people stood around trying to be customers. On September 1, the opening day of waterfowl season, the store was manned by a skeleton crew of women.

New friends had invited me and I was hot. I had a twelve gauge side by side that had knocked off a fair number of turkeys, whitetails and squirrels but if notched for each flying bird brought down wouldn't have been much marred. In fact a dozen seasons later, when my gun cabinet was locked for the last time my title was forever recorded with hunting pals as, "The worst wing in the West." Our insensitive wag even suggested that instead of gun and labrador, my interest might be better served with a cane and German shepherd.

We were headed for an almost secret place forty miles east of Anchorage, the Hayfield Flats. For a week before, my buddies never spoke this name above a whisper and only then after clandestine looks in all directions. Remarkable my fortune to have fallen into this expedition. And with all the ducks rumored to be 'in', big northern birds, maybe my companions would be too busy to notice my miserable shooting. The limit was six ducks. I bought eighty shells.

We arrived pre dawn at a narrow dirt road leading to the walking trail that drops over the edge of a hill overlooking the flats. The road, about three quarters of a mile long, gave us our first problem. It was so jammed with camper vehicles of hunters who had spent the night that we had to park beside the highway and walk the trail. By the time we started down the traversing path leading to the famed flats we were in the longest line of armed men I had seen since Korea. Reaching the swampy lowlands and looking back toward the hill, hundreds of lit cigarettes, in ceaseless procession, bobbed and glowed in a descending crisscross resembling the evacuation of Pekin. I've seen less attendance at national soccer games in Chile.

At sun-up the killing began, ceaseless shotgun blasts deafening. There were fist fights over dead ducks, the acrid smell of burned powder hung heavy over the morning and yet through it all by nine o'clock most gunners left the battle with limit filled game bags. I even managed my six before eleven and came away with most of my fourth box of shells. Amazing! My first hunt in wilderness Alaska.

Well there was a wild last frontier and bit by bit I found it. By November when my wife flew over Cook Inlet from Anchorage and shot a moose, fifty dollars for a guaranteed kill, we had a rented standup freezer locker filled with enough late run silver salmon, Dolly Varden, ducks, rabbits, spruce grouse, moose and caribou, so that except for bacon, we bought no meat for a year. It was as close as I ever came to a real subsistence lifestyle. Then it satisfied something wild in me, yet it, in time, ended my blood lust. My predator instinct found expression but the carnage was too much.

When I say carnage, it wasn't just my own, the Alaskan hunting mentality created the worst of all the negative things said about hunting. There were no ethics. I walked over six carcasses that had been killed and left to rot on my first caribou hunt. Three men in a bar laughed about being drunk, shooting a cow moose nine times, including blowing off her front legs, before she died. I don't know why they didn't kill me for throwing my beer in their faces. And through the kitchen window of a three hundred thousand dollar Anchorage Orthodontist's home I saw rotting geese laying in his backyard as he demanded assurances of returning from a fishing trip with me with full limits, his and mine. Over-indulging my predator instinct destroyed the life from gorgeous fellow creatures until blood saturated my soul. I had to stop!

All my chase joys at last channelled into one deep flow—fly fishing.

Somewhere along the path from cat-like fascination with all creatures considered game, satisfaction only coming with the kill, evolving to a time when fulfillment depends on leaving the field with all players as unharmed as when the play began, may be a step from barbarity to civility (I know how close civility rhymes with senility). Twenty years of the Alaskan outdoor blood bath and my participation in it brought me to that point.

Yet many of my most cherished thoughts and feelings now still come from recollections of the hunt. I have few memories more pleasant than evening campfire coals glowing under frying pans filled with moose liver, deer back strap and yes—freshly killed trout. In fact it might help relieve our collective pomposity a bit if every catch and release fly angler as holy ritual, had to kill, clean, cook and eat a fish now and then, perhaps the first catch of the season, just to stay reminded of what we're all about.

Though the two hundred thousand visitors and another hundred thousand resident anglers that crowd almost every easily accessible stream bank during the short Alaskan fishing season, diminish the esthetic aspect of the experience once available, it's still the most remarkable sport fishery in the world. I found her a magnificent, grand, yet delicate young woman, fresh, virginal and I fell deep in love. And as sure as I am filled with the wonders she gave me, as a writer/photographer I must live with the guilt of having kissed and told. Here's something from the best of those days.

The morning was sparkling clear. We were flying at seven thousand five hundred feet a few miles south of Mount Iliamna.

Chris Clarke, noted watercolorist, with Kenai River Dolly Varden.

Iliamna is ten thousand and sixteen feet high, a hundred and fifteen miles southwest of Anchorage, Alaska. Few mountains rival it for beauty. Still a live volcano and snow-capped year-round, on a bright day like this one it dominates the vast Alaska Range with breathtaking splendor. I never see or recall this awesome natural monument without thinking of Monica and Harry and a precious secret they shared with me.

She was twenty nine, blond and lovely of figure and face. A bright young woman who after years of international flying had been appointed a senior flight attendant. Harry her husband was thirty two, tall, lean and handsome. A quiet, pleasant man with thick, wavy, ink black hair.

*Mike Cusack float plane,
King Salmon Lodge.*

He was gentle of manner yet presided over a thriving bank in Dallas, Texas. Among other things they shared a passion for fly fishing and had enjoyed much of the best. Now they had made it to North America's finest—Alaska.

Still more than that, after five long days in constant company with them, I discovered that ten years of marriage had created a love affair as near perfect as any romantic writer could imagine. In those days I had given up believing matrimony could do that, so it was turning out a remarkable time for me. I was their guide.

They really were each other's best friend. As we flew around from one day's angling to another their teasing, not cutting or harsh, was a warm source of fun. Never a 'put down' it was more a way of saying:

"Hey! You don't need to put up any fronts. Relax and be yourself and when you do something foolish trust me to share that part of you too."

They had somehow developed an ability to support without intruding, share without over-stepping and care without smothering. Here is a case in point, one of many.

We decided to try for Arctic char on our third morning out. The first day, Monday, had been a rainbow trout bonanza with a dozen fish, each well over six pounds (and one over twelve) landed, photographed and released with gentle care. Our quest for silver salmon on Tuesday had required a two hour flight to Kodiak Island but was dream-like. Five hours of windy fly casting turned up twenty four bright, sea run scrappers that gobbled streamer flies like kids munching popcorn. From eight to fourteen pounds they cleared the water between reel screaming runs, two or three times each.

Now it was Wednesday and we were flaring in over a stretch of water I knew held several char in the ten pound class. As the pilot eased the floats onto a wide place in the stream, water erupted on both sides with schools of large fish. My client's eyes glistened with excitement.

"Ooh! Honey look, there are so many." The lady's voice was low but charged. Her husband smiled.

Back then I wasn't clever enough to insist that rods be cased in transit no matter how short the ride and as Monica stepped from the float somehow Harry's new custom graphite rod found its way under her foot. For those who have heard that $400 crunch, the sound is unforgettable. For guides who have worked much with couples incidents like this often promise even more notable noises. I froze.

"Hey! It's okay! Things like that happen. Remember when I backed the car over your bicycle? Come on kid, we'll share your rod."

She was upset, not Harry. He only wanted to calm her and get on with fishing. I was impressed, yet there was more to come. The tundra trail to the wading point was narrow. You needed to put one foot just so in front of the other to avoid tripping. So when the husband saw a large, brilliantly colored char roll on the surface he missed his footing, lurched forward, tried to recover and fell backward into his wife. More than that, he crashed into her rod. The snap was louder than the crunch.

To my wonder they put their arms around each other, laughed for a long while and then Harry looked up.

"Jim, do people on these trips ever just say 'to hell with it' for a day and go back to the lodge for lunch and maybe spend the afternoon getting a little crocked?" It sounded good to me.

They had spare rods and so did I so the rest of the week went fine, lots of adventure, lots of fish. And the afternoon crocking brought us together in a special way that sometimes happens between clients and guides. We spent the remaining evenings in my cabin away from the lodge. Pleasant suppers, a shared bottle or two and mellow conversations. Great! I was sad when the last evening came.

The only fish they hadn't caught were grayling and since our flight back to Anchorage wasn't until afternoon we agreed to get up early and take the Jeep to a nearby stream where there were many of these big-finned beauties. As they got up to return to the lodge, Monica said:

"Jim, we have a secret we want to share. We found out just before this trip and we haven't told anyone else yet." We were all smiling as they left.

Morning dawned in a steady, drizzling rain with westerly winds beginning. We didn't care. Thick sweaters and rain gear made it almost pleasant and several long fat grayling made it worthwhile. But the storm grew worse and worse. By the time we returned to the lodge, had showers and a hot lunch, the wind was blowing a gale. At the end of the meal I spoke with the couple.

"I really don't like this weather. Why don't you just stay over one more day, relax and rest up for your trip home?"

"Sounds fine," Harry smiled, "but impossible! I have a board meeting on Monday that simply can't happen without me."

I had serious misgivings though it was obvious he was firm. I spoke to the lodge manager and had him cancel my ticket. The weather wasn't any worse than a hundred other times I flew in Alaska. If you wait for good flying conditions there, you will stay where you are—a lot, but I was tired, wanted to rest, so why not?

The wind had let up some as passengers boarded the twin otter that afternoon though visibility was lessening. I didn't envy my friends their trip. At best it would be a bumpy ride. Harry and I hugged and Monica kissed my cheek. We agreed to stay in touch, to fish together again, somewhere, sometime. One often says these things and yet I thought perhaps this time we really would. There was a tear in her eye, mine too. And then they roared off into the rain clouds.

It wasn't until 10 o'clock that night when we received word that the plane hadn't arrived in Anchorage. I began to pray. And not until midnight when they located the wreckage at seven thousand five hundred feet in a crevasse on Mount Iliamna, only an electronic beeper alive to tell the tale. I began to drink.

Before I passed into a merciful stupor I tried to puzzle it out. Maybe, I reasoned, the time to go is when you are at the very best point in your life. After all, who can know what's to come. I know this couple had no inkling of the crash. Probably holding hands, their common habit, probably asleep, her head on his shoulder and then the lights went out. Yet their secret always haunts me.

"Jim," she radiated with more beauty than our dinner candles, "We've been married for ten years and finally I'm pregnant."

"The first men that our Saviour dear
Did choose to wait upon him here
Blest fishers were, and fish the last
Food was that he on earth did taste
I therefore strive to follow those
Whom he to follow him hath chose."

— Izaak Walton, 1653. ▦

Kathy Repine with coho salmon.

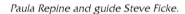

Paula Repine and guide Steve Ficke.

5

BEJEWELED TROUT
AND ROSE RED FUCHSIA

*T*he hopper leaped high for a lone green leaf hanging from a limb near the water. A gust of wind swept down from the mountain. He struck the current's surface with a-plop! He tried to hop free but couldn't break loose from the stream. A large long shadow appeared beneath him, bulged the surface slightly and in an instant they were gone.

I have never made much money in the sport fishing business, not many do. A few of the better lodge operators finish fairly well off, there are one or two writers who have done well, a couple of photographers, some shop owners, a handful of booking agents and an occasional tackle representative.

But if your daughter came home one night and announced that she had taken up with a fishing writer, it would not be cause to assume that your old age was now secure. Yet here I was, thirty thousand feet over Jamaica, a lovely Chilean flight attendant handing me a scotch and soda, on my way to sample exotic angling somewhere south of a place called Puerto Montt, Chile.

It was my third day of steady travel, having just returned to Alaska from the Tokyo Fishing Show, ten hours in Anchorage to do laundry, twelve hours flying to Miami and now into the first of ten more (hours not scotches) to Santiago. But I was more excited than I had been since I went to the Gaspe Peninsula the first time two years before. You have to be careful about turning something you love into your profession. You can get jaded. Another fishing trip? Ho hum! I have seen it but it has not gotten me yet. Still, some trips are more intriguing than others and what time I had used to bone up on southern Chile, had me aroused.

"You're going to find Alaska twenty years ago!" Mel Krieger, the famed fly casting instructor, who has spent a good deal of time in neighboring Argentina, said on the phone before he launched into a detailed rundown of necessary gear and methods.

"Whoa!" I laughed. "I'm going there to photograph. I won't fish more than an hour or two. I'll have a couple of pack rods, a handful of flies, maybe two reels but it's pictures and an article I'm after." I listened anyway. Krieger knows his stuff.

At the time Alaska twenty years back was when I arrived there and what an adventure it turned out to be. In fact it's still happening, yet the opportunity to see someplace new, fish new waters with new challenges, experience other cultures in other languages, are all aspects of angling that keep my arteries open. I often tried to explain to my mother that even if I had taken up something legitimate, that paid well, I would have blown the money anyway—fishing.

There is no doubt that Chile is a long way from the United States but there is a component of the trip that eases the pain. Chilean airlines go out of their way to make your trip a comfortable one, plus Ladeco, the one I was on, seated ninety people in the same space U.S. carriers jam a hundred and twenty six. The food and drink service was superb, never ending and with a snooze or two and a first run movie thrown in, we made Santiago before real agony got to us.

I read about travel, a lot, and do a fair amount of it. It sharpens my image of a place before arriving, though twice in my life I have been jolted by how inaccurate my preconceptions were. My first arrival in Japan, forty years ago, polluted with the lingering effects of World War II propaganda was like that and again upon moving to Alaska, after reading everything I could find for over a year. Both places turned out so different and so much better than I had expected. Now there have been three such times.

Chile in general, Santiago in particular, is delightful. In this capital metropolis of six million I had somehow expected soldiers with uzis patrolling streets filled with repressed, abjectly poor people. My blurry vision was of a politically unhappy, poverty stricken country where a few landed gentry lived like the Barons of old. How in the name of God does that crap get around?

This country is a blessed land, gorgeous from snow-capped mountains, across lush fertile valleys, to a lovely seacoast extending from close to the Equator south for three thousand miles. The people are pleasant, well clothed and fed and there is no more

Chilca (wild fuchsia), another common wildflower of southern Chile.
FACING PAGE: Chilean kingfisher.
PAGES 32 & 33: Valley of the Kings en route to Futaleufu Lodge.

BEJEWELED TROUT AND ROSE RED FUCHSIA

Mel Krieger, famous casting instructor
and writer.

Oxen, the most common farm vehicle in
southern Chile.

oppression here than elected governments bureaucracies create anywhere else. When I first arrived Penochet's dictatorship was in its last years yet even then political discussion was open, pro and con. No one seemed hesitant to express all variety of opinions to me.

Shops were filled with goods, everyone seemed to be buying and food markets and restaurants were exceptional. The country is renowned for its wine. In the countryside or in downtown Santiago I felt safer and was treated kinder than in any U.S. community I have been in lately. What can I say?

There was a marvelous sunset over the Pacific just before we landed at Santiago. In Miami I had been joined by a couple of other anglers heading to the same lodge. One of my two new friends, Bill Douglass an anthropologist from the University of Nevada, was asleep, maybe comatose from the volume of food we had enjoyed. The other, Mike Michalak, was engrossed in a book. My thoughts wafted off.

How many other times had I been so thrilled at the beginning of an angling adventure? Many dedicated anglers take up collecting. Assortments of old rods, early reels, flies from the past, etc., become as precious to them as the sport itself. When you see these carefully gathered treasures in the hands of someone who loves them you appreciate how they feel, because all of us who find it important to spend time in the appealing surroundings of fishing are fellow collectors, if only of priceless memories.

That first time on the Grande Cascapedia, backpacking the Bitterroot/Selway Wilderness, wading the mountain streams of Hokkaido and all those first times to most of Alaska's fabled water. Snook and tarpon, now so long ago. So many first times and here it was again.

After a refreshing night in a Santiago hotel we jetted a short hop to Puerto Montt, transferring to an even shorter commuter flight further south to a small village called La Junta. Then by

van for an hour or so to the tiny town of Puyuhuapi. Termas Lodge was a quick boat ride from there. We arrived in time for lunch, fishing by early afternoon.

Lodges come in various sizes, shapes and quality levels. They are after all only places to eat and sleep between fishing days, yet the tone of your stay begins and ends there. From the time we rounded a point and received our first look at the place, if aesthetics mattered we were in for a happy week. Buildings were clustered on a high green knoll overlooking a sheltered saltwater cove. Dense clusters of wild, rose-hued fuchsias hung down from thickets in every direction. The dining room had a huge picture window with a panorama of water and mountains beyond. The staff, mostly Chilean, was on the dock to meet and greet us and it would have been difficult not to have felt like visiting royalty.

The luggage vanished not to be seen again until we were shown to our cabins where it reappeared. Cabin was a misnomer, it was an A-frame chalet, attractive, furnished with wicker. In one corner was a large copper, free-standing fireplace where cheery fires were blazing when we returned from fishing, after dinner and upon waking in the morning. There was a bathroom with the largest tile tub I have ever seen and most important, we slept on comfortable beds. And you know what else?

At the end of a trail leading around the cove, less than fifty yards from my front door, with a view of everything were steamy warm bathing pools fed by natural hot springs. Think about it! After a long day of travel or wading rocky streams or hours spent standing in cold river water? Hmmmm!

All this with excellent Chilean food, pre-pared and served as in a fine dining salon, and . . . by now you are saying, "Yeah, yeah, but what about the fishing?" For me that turned out best of all.

Jim Repine with Futaleufu brown trout.
Ron Meek photo

Our first outing was by boat from the lodge, thirty minutes to the mouth of the Queualt River in quest of sea run brown trout. The weather was near perfect, temperature in the mid sixties patchy clouds, not enough wind to interfere with casting but enough to keep mosquitoes at bay. Except, now get this, there were no mosquitoes, not a few, not any. No mosquitoes, poisonous snakes, black flies, sand flies, nothing except a few slow witted horse flies that were easy to swat. I know now there is an occasional mosquito in Chile but so rare, these little devils that have pursued me across every other continent, that I go entire seasons here without taking insect repellent from my fishing vest pocket. Either no one locally has sinned or God doesn't realize that people have made it this far south already. Whatever, there are few unpleasant critters in this part of the world.

Mike was very aggressive on the water and he came prepared with a 'not exactly secret' weapon, a pancora crab imitation. It looked a lot like a large, orange, weighted nymph with peculiar, shiny feelers; to me that is. To a brown trout just in from the sea, it must have resembled a pancora crab because we were not all that long on the river before Mike made his way upstream and drew first blood.

"Boy! They hit hard and then really move out." He was grinning, solid into his second fish by the time I caught up. "Try right over there just under that overhang."

Sea run brown? Talk about something new, the silvery three pounder Mike had just

Brown trout.

released was the first one I had ever seen. These are not the large ten to twenty pound fish that are reputed to spawn in these waters during the August winter, a time when fishing is closed. In truth, I still have no first hand knowledge of whether this run is fact or legend. Yet I was wired enough as I dropped a weighted Olive Muddler into the spot and dead drifted it as I had seen my friend do. Nothing! I did it again. Still nothing!

"Wow!" Came my pal's yell as his third fish, larger than either of the other two, was wildly running upriver. "Look at that fish go!" He bellowed back over his shoulder. "I have plenty of these crabs. Want one?"

Did I want one of those funny looking crab patterns? "You bet. Hurry up and release that guy and dig another one out." There are times when I am easy.

And it worked! My second cast with the pancora and—bam! Though this was the smallest of the lot, less than three pounds, it was my first and put a hard bend in my six weight graphite as it streaked off downriver. These were tough fish.

The river narrowed just up from the mouth and, except for the difference in the trees along the bank, could have passed for a stream on the Oregon coast. A soft gravel bottom in the shallow runs made wading pleasant with good deep holes at the bends. I can't describe the fish as prolific, though there were plenty for an afternoon's sport. But I shouldn't go much longer without mentioning L.A. Gillette. Yet there is an incident from my coon hunting days that should be related first.

I once was slickered by a dog dealer into buying an old coon hound by his story of how good this once fine hunter would be for training my puppies. It sounded reasonable until I took Major to the woods the first night. A detail the man had left out was that the elderly bluetick was as deaf as a tree. Once loose and off hunting there was not the slightest hope of calling him back and no better odds of finding him again anytime soon. As an elder tutor his value was decreased a tad in that you could only put his hard won wisdom to use about every third night, with the inevitable two days in between it took to walk the woods until you found him.

Even then I would feel like some heartless animal abuser as he would look at me with those big sad hound dog eyes as if to say:

"Thanks, you jerk. You brought me out here last Thursday night, walked off and left me and here it is Saturday afternoon? What do you think, because I am old I don't need food?"

After three or four outings I retired the old boy for the good hound he had been with free run of the farm and all the Purina he could eat. He even found a clever way to indulge his life long love of hunting and yet accommodate the rigors of aging that increasingly beset him.

There was a huge groundhog, as old as the dog and almost as shrewd, that lived under our barn. He had resided there for years and with dozens of dogs, beagles and blueticks that came and went through those years, none came close to catching him though all had tried.

The critter's secret lie in his constant state of alertness. He would wander out from his deeply dug sanctuary never keeping his head down to eat long enough to give an enemy time to outrun him to his hole. Any hint of movement in his direction and the chuck would bolt to the barn with blurring speed and vanish into the ground. Major decided two things: One that he would have this groundhog and two that he would take all the time he needed to do it.

Every day for weeks the hound lay as still as a stone, snoozing through the long summer days as older gentlemen are prone to do, yet if you observed closely you would have noted that each day or two he slept a little nearer to the groundhog's den. And as surely as all things come to those who wait, there came an afternoon when all the grandfather hound had to do was stand up, move a step or two and pen the intercepted groundhog to the ground. It was Major's last kill, he died himself a short while after.

We were joined in Santiago by a certain Mr. Lawrence A. Gillette, a gentleman in his seventies from Idaho. Not just from the great potato state he was a lifelong spud farmer himself. On his lapel he sported an oversize button that proclaimed "50 years in Potatoes."

L.A., as he prefers to be called was in good shape, fine shape in fact, though he didn't move as spryly as he once did. I was to learn things from him as the week continued. Like at the end of that first afternoon after the rest of us had paraded up and down the river as far as time would allow, L.A. didn't move more than ten yards from his first cast. He released as many fish as the rest of us and like my old dog Major, persistence rewarded him with the unquestioned fish of the day, a six or seven pound trout. L.A. was my roommate.

I don't write well enough to amply describe what the hot springs felt like that evening, I'm not sure anyone could. I melded into a flowing pool of hot mineral water, amid flowering fuchsias, effects of scotch and soda and thoughts of other baths in the misty isles of Nippon. I was still feeling the vibrant pull of a sea trout, of which before this same afternoon I had only read about, and all with a ravenous anticipation of dinner. At Termas this evening ritual made leaving an afternoon angling hot spot almost worth it.

Our first dinner was some succulent, small saltwater fish, battered and broiled. They came with fresh baked, oven warm bread, boiled potatoes, a fresh garden salad, a tasty, dry Chilean white wine and served with quiet elegance. Though even that did not turn out to be my high point of the day. It was at dinner that a new character entered the play.

Bo Ivonovich was a tall, handsome Englishman, Ivonovich not withstanding. For me, there is something right, reassuring if you will, about Englishmen angling with flies. I make no comment on the vices or virtues of their other worldwide influences over the past century but there is one thing certain, wherever they went, fly fishing soon took root. New Zealand and Australia are famous examples but the British effect in Patagonia is not so well known. And how many people are aware that the Crown's own diplomats introduced modern fly angling to Japan before World War II?

In any event we had a splendid and lively conversation. I questioned and listened as Bo had pandered to his angling addiction all over the globe. After coffee and some delicious pastry, I went to bed and fell into one of those deep, deep, at peace with all, slumbers that seem to last for a moment or two and then it's morning.

The next day we flew. Termas had one of the two amphibian airplanes registered in Chile at the time, a Cessna 206, such a phenomenon to local people that they sometimes turned out when they heard it, looked up, pointed and talked about the boat that flew.

We spent the day on another gorgeous river named Aldunate where Mike lost a resident brown he felt exceeded ten pounds. I spent most of the time photographing and kibitzing with my English friend while he cast his fourteen foot rod. There is a chapter or two just on those long European rods but suffice it to say, they are a different concept than most of us know yet beautiful to watch in the hands of someone like Bo Ivonovich. It was disappointing to discover that he would be leaving the lodge in the morning.

Puyuhuapi vista.

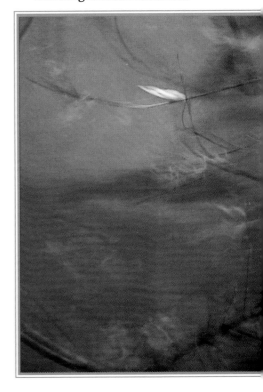

Trout image beneath the surface.

Rainbow trout.

The next day found us on a large mountain lake, Lago Copa, where once we had the plane secured at the beach, L.A. got into a float tube and began casting to some reeds along the shore. I wandered up the inflow stream and Mike and Bill headed for the boca, the wadeable underwater delta where the inflow stream drops off into the lake. At mid morning L.A. was skunked, I had released a couple of small rainbows and the other two found the glory hole.

By the time I joined Bill and Mike they had released about twenty rainbows each with one fish in excess of eight pounds. It was a matter of a long cast, a sink tip or sinking head, counting long enough to assure a large Woolly Bugger or Leech had ample time to sink and then retrieving the fly in a swimming motion. One had to move the fly quickly, striking at the slightest tug, otherwise the chance of deep hooking, resulting in a dead fish was too great. Even with the cherries already picked I caught another three on an Olive Matuka and just before lunch L.A. found his way over and managed to hook two more. By standards anywhere, boca fishing that morning was hot.

After lunch we moved to a small stream flowing between two lakes, perhaps a mile and a half long and as pretty as any I have seen. I had decided that dries were all I wanted to fish for the remainder of the trip, the water looked prime and I knew about cherry picking myself. I hit the gravel in motion and made it a hundred yards downstream ahead of my friends, before starting a number twelve Royal Wulff through its first drift. It didn't make it far. One of the most uniquely colored two pound rainbows I have found, gulped the fly and leaped straight up as only rainbows do.

For the next two hours I was in heaven. I didn't count. About every third drift brought a rise. Some I missed, some got off and I released a bunch. All things considered, aesthetics, the company, the weather and those green-hued trout, it was far better than this angler deserved.

We all had good angling. Bill fished dry all afternoon also and appeared to have a fish on every time I looked up. I have never soaked in hot springs with a happier group than that evening. My notes, written later that night were as follows:

"Brown trout, brook trout (Mike had two from the lake), and rainbows in fascinating circumstances. We are finding plenty of fish, far more than anglers need to satiate catch lusts, though I am convinced that it is only because of lack of pressure. I have watched Alaska's fishery for twenty years. I know what pressure can do and how quick, and this is a country without benefit of massive salmon runs. The natural preservatives of difficult access will only slow the depletion of these fish as it has in Alaska, but the potential for irreparable harm is even greater here.

"Today I waded a stream as intriguing as they get. No airplane flew over, no other anglers appeared and I was able for a time to indulge an inner tugging to re-enter an unpeopled environment. I need that now and then. Don't get the idea that it's anti-human. The other circumstance I most love is a man-made downtown. What is distasteful for me is all the compromised suburban mediocrity in between. But in the 586,000 square miles that is Alaska, pristine moments are now difficult to find. Is that what's coming here? Dare I publish the truth about southern Chile?"

I took the fourth day off, organized my notes and visited 'downtown' Puyuhuapi with one of the lodge owners, Steve Currey. He is a fine young man with a love and respect for Chile and the Chileans. And I also tried to get a slant on just what to write regarding things here. "To call a place Paradise is to spell its doom." That is an old adage I try to keep as a journalistic first commandment yet the ingredients for heaven vary a lot from one person to another. I also confess to having honored one of the Latin world's best customs by sneaking in a little siesta around three o'clock. Not a bad day!

The hot spring's pre dinner communion that evening was spiked with a liturgy about super brown trout fishing my friends enjoyed in the afternoon. Mike held a fish in his hands that they agreed was the trip monster.

We were joined at dinner by a new arrival, another young Englishman, Philip Wright, who turned out to be as pleasant as his fellow countryman Bo. A capital lot of anglers those English. It was also later that night, back in our cabin, that I got to know my roommate better.

During one of my mindless tirades on the imminent collapse of America and all things of value, and about the time I was convinced that L.A.'s staunch patriotism was a 'head in the sand' product of fifty years with potatoes or whatever, this grandfather of twenty eight children handed me something to read. His daughter, a professional journalist, had compiled it.

The article was the old gentleman's account, in his own words, of his ghastly experiences as a Nazi prisoner of war, the heart wrenching details of the deaths of many of his closest friends, his escape and for me the most moving, his letters to his wife throughout the ordeal. It was the perfect cure for my raving. Funny, you never know about the quiet ones. The next day my roomy and I fished away from the others. And the following is proof that God still blesses fools and knaves.

Bo delivered the other three anglers to some far off hot spot and then returned for us. He flew us to a lake too windy for casting so we headed up the inflow stream which turned out to be the big brown trout water of the day before. My partner stayed close to the mouth with his eye on the boca in case the wind began to still. I strayed a half mile or so upstream. I was alone in the wilds of Chile. When I made it far enough for the trees along the bank to block most of the wind, there was a long stretch of riffles as fishy looking as one could imagine. For a long time I just stood still, looking, listening and longing for more time, my backpack and Jubal my dog. At last I began to fish. And then it happened.

It came on my last fishing day. A fish somewhere between six and eight pounds, encrusted with rubies and other sparkling gems, a brown trout, not a young one, in vivid colors. It took a ginked Madam X that a dear friend, Karel Bauer, bought for me from John Foust, the noted Montana tier. I would like to tell you that I recall every fish I have ever caught, they were all that precious, yet I cannot. Nor do I want to believe I am ever callous about these marvelous creatures that have filled my life with so much joy and priceless adventure, though I sometimes am. But not this time. I won't forget this exquisite Chilean brown trout.

Neither will I cease being haunted by visions of virgin bamboo forests and tall coyhues against mist shrouded, snow-capped mountains, wildflowers glowing in patches of sunlight, streams, rivers and lakes, beauty beyond description, flowing through a thousand valleys. I also never found a city, town or village there not enchanting enough for me to want to linger for a time.

Shangri La retains its magic because of immunity from corruption. It's only a dream. But in the south of Chile there exists a real yet fragile environment offering mid winter escape to where February is like August though it's with heart-felt reticence I relate this much. It's the same compromise I have made for more than twenty years about Alaska with lingering uneasiness over the results. And while I would have closed the gate behind me when I crossed into that wonderland, the reality of my profession is sharing good fortunes with those who read. Still I have misgivings.

"For Angling is somewhat like Poetry, men are to be born so: I mean with inclinations to it, though they both may be heightened by discourse and practice."

—Izaak Walton, 1653. ✳

Fall in Patagonia.

Joan Wulff with a Futaleufu rainbow.

6

THEY LAUGHED AT ME

*T*he evening light was fading as the big dragonfly continued swooping close enough to the lake's silver black surface to deposit its eggs. On its third skimming run over the same spot the water exploded as a four pound brown trout splashed up to grab it in mid air.

"Mr. Raypeen?" The flight steward surprised me by using my name, pronunciation not withstanding. "The Captain has invited you to the flight deck!"

We were two hours out of San Francisco en route to Sydney, via Honolulu and the steady hum of jet engines had lulled me to sleep. I managed a foggy smile and answered:

"A huh. . .it's Ree pine. . .like replanting a pine tree." I corrected while getting up to follow.

It was my first summons to a flight deck. As we entered the cockpit of the Qantas Jumbo jet two things struck me. The space allotted for controlling such a mammoth airship is tiny, yet there are hundreds of lights, soft white, green, red, overhead, on both sides and mixed among glowing instruments. The entire first year of flight school must go to learning this myriad of signals. This added to millions of stars visible through the surrounding windows, horizon to horizon on a clear Pacific evening, I felt transported to the eerie realm of outer space.

"This is Mr. Raypeen, a magazine writer." The steward introduced me a bit like one announces the distasteful presence of the next door neighbor's kid.

"Jim. . .ah. . .just call me Jim." There! I had the bugger and we both knew it as the Captain, his co pilot and the navigator each shook my hand.

"What will you be writing about down under?" They wanted to know and like so many other times in my life, the next word won me an instant O.K.

"Fishing!" I smiled.

An hour later I hadn't spoken twenty words, my dinner was served there and my newest fishing buddies were still sharing all they knew about our common pastime. Only the navigator was a fly fisherman, the other two preferring surf casting and ocean bottom fishing but it was all fascinating for me. The tone was set for the eight weeks to come.

I alternated for the rest of the flight between eating, sleeping, drinking, movies, eating, sleeping, drinking and more of the same. It is a long trip.

Though I was to come back later for leisure days in Sydney now it was just a glimpse from the air of this fine city as we circled to land with a short time in the airport. Then a commuter flight towards Cancoban and the home of a certain Mike Spry, guide, writer and pal. But something nice happened between the next airport and Mike.

A year or two before, I had hosted this saucy cherub in Alaska. He was interested in booking Australian clients for opposite season adventures. Our time together turned out magic, a grand tour of fishing lodges and late night Anchorage bars. It was during the closing months of my, "Two pints a day keeps nice girls away", single years. Now I would see the 'Tiny Tiger' in his home den. What's big about this man is his spirit.

But before we reunited I met Margaret his wife. "Marg", she's known by in the incessant Australian aversion to pronouncing all of any word's syllables. Barbecues are barbys, post office boxes are po boxes, etc. And in that vein Marg is a beaut. She was my charming and most informative guide for the three hour drive to their home. My eyes grew wider the farther we went.

Australia, at least the part leading through the Murray River Valley and into the Snowy Mountains, is as beautiful an environment as I have seen. Rolling green hills reaching higher the closer you get to the mountains, vast grazing stations (ranches) with grand herds of well bred cattle and sheep, big Montana-like sky, panoramas extending for distant miles at times in four directions and most impressive of all, the ever-present eucalyptus. There are over five hundred varieties of eucalyptus on the continent though it's huge red gums towering over everything along the river bottom that gives the place its distinctive appearance. It's a scenic marvel.

The Snowy Mountains aren't the high rugged Andes of my beloved Chile. More akin to the Blue Ridge range that I grew up near, they first appeared over the horizon as hazy cloud formations. The movie, "The Man From Snowy River", had been a good one for me, adapted from a famous folk poem, I recalled that it was filmed in these same hills. If eucalyptus had grown in Texas it would be hard to separate scenes of Australia's white conquest from its counterpoint epic of North America's west, horses, cattlemen, sheepmen, the lot. Only the Aussie's aborigines were less combative. This was where my outback adventures would take place.

Cancoban was neat, a village more than a town, painted houses, planted and tended yards, a few stores, a country club, about five hundred people and from any point about a ten minute walk to the Swampy Plains River inhabited by a generous population of aggressive, fat brown trout. The Spry home was there, my cheery hearth in a foreign land and for eight weeks my permanent address. On arriving that first afternoon, Marg said:

"I think we'd best just drop off your luggage Jim and then drive to the bridge. Mike should be arriving there soon to end his float trip."

It's always a marvelous thing to be in a new surrounding and see a familiar face. My friend rounded a final bend in the river and beamed when he saw me, my own grin a match. We had really become "mites" (mates) in our short few weeks in Alaska.

"Hello! Now, who is this Yank?" One of his clients stepped out of the raft and offered his hand as the guide secured the boat to a root. There must be unfriendly blokes

Jumbo jet cockpit.
FACING PAGE: Grasshopper imitation.

THEY LAUGHED AT ME

41

Sydney.

somewhere on a continent this large yet I never ran into one. The other angler was just as open as they described their day's adventures. A beautiful float, enough brown trout in the 14 to 18 inch class to keep everyone happy and all taken on hopper patterns. Sounded just right to me.

"This Yank is me 'mite' from Alaska!" Mike explained as he half lifted, half dragged the twelve foot boat out of the water. For the first time in twenty years it struck me then that I probably was no longer from Alaska.

"I'm not sure about that old friend." I chuckled. "You know I've been back to Chile for a second trip, three months this time and, well, I don't know but I might just be your mate from Chile now."

There wasn't an unpleasant or uneventful day for the next two months. The country was in the grips of a summer-long drought and while critical for the local sheep and cattle industry, it created ideal weather and angling conditions. There was an endless sequence of long sunny days, clouds of hoppers in fields that lined most of the river's banks, enough wind to put a constant supply of this prime trout bait on the water and me with nothing to do but fish and photograph. A bucolic season is an apt description.

Mike had me floating with him the next morning, yet not at any painful hour. At tea (supper) that first night my schooling began.

"There's no point going to the river before the sun gets the hoppers up and moving. We could catch the odd fish on other patterns but hoppers are what they want, so why fight nature?" After the exhausting trip to get there it was pleasing not to hear the usual cruel news about pre dawn departures. "There's not much to know if you have already fished from moving rafts." He continued. "Only to put the hopper on the water with a pronounced slap, the same as they hit when the wind slams them down."

Two or three spring seasons on Montana's Bitterroot River floating with George Gehrke had taught me the moving raft routine. You must always be looking downriver for the next cast, planning your presentation in time or most of the best opportunities slip by unfished. There is a special knack to it though the hopeless shock of missing the first few hot spots tends to sharpen you quickly. And a fair number of my casts smacked the water. Many fish or not it's always fast action. My first day's float on the Swampy Plains had plenty of both.

We covered several miles of water from below the impoundment dam to just short of the confluence with the famed Murray River. This stretch is an idyllic mix of riffles, slicks and pools, superb water clarity, pleasant wading bars and a tree-lined panorama of eucalyptus and giant weeping willows.

The latter, planted to prevent bank erosion, impart a genteel feeling of moving through an old southern Georgia plantation yet it's never far before a great, tall red gum brings you back to the land of marsupials.

Australia has an infinite number of critters with pouches. From tiny field mouse size to mammoth kangaroos and one of the hundreds even comes duck-billed platypus but more of that guy later. As far as I observed, the trout, having come over from England with the rabbits and foxes were without this peculiarity, yet I shouldn't doubt that a few thousand years from now even troutlings may peer from mummy's tummys like everything else there.

The water wasn't big, between a large creek and small river, you could get your mental arms around it—in general figure it out. It was comfortable from the beginning. Fish were where they should be, doing what they should be doing but I had surprises to come and lessons to learn. After twenty years in Alaska's fishery, more bountiful than good angling need be but with not the first brown trout my initial lesson came early.

"Jim, put your fly over this next flat and let it drift ahead of the raft. There that's it! Just right!" I followed the instruction with a total lack of faith.

Sight fishing is often the method in Alaska and I felt I had become pretty good at it over the years. Rivers like Katmai's Brooks for example, crowded with fresh sockeye salmon, large rainbows mixed among them are prime grounds for honing your ability to translate watery shapes and forms into this fish or that. Distinguishing a silver salmon resting within a thick mingling of sockeye, chum and pinks can many times be the key to success during most of August on a multitude of rivers throughout the Iliamna/Bristol Bay drainages and my friend was having me drift a fly over a run with a foot of water so clear that every rock and pebble was in plain sight. If there was anything larger than a minnow I couldn't miss it and I saw zero fish. Nothing!

The strike was like seeing a ghost. Impossible, yet happening, a fat sixteen incher with a pretty good splash had munched my Hopper and was hell bent toward the deeper water on the other side of the racing river. I would call it bedlamic—if there were such a word.

PACIFIC RIM FLY FISHING: THE UNREPENTANT PREDATOR

42

Repine walking the outback.
FACING PAGE: Snowy Mountain stream.

Not long after that a seven pounder, the largest of the trip, put tackle and me through brown trout boot camp. Mike had to beach the raft to deal with this guy. The fish had taken so lightly that when I first lifted the rod I thought the fly was snagged. Then the snag detonated and went wild, running downriver quicker than the fast floating inflatable could follow. The line was well into backing before he made his first jump and decided to reverse direction. A while later as I held this precious creature up for a fast photo, Kookaburra begin laughing from high atop a nearby red gum. Their voices sounded too human. Their timing too exact, not to imagine they had watched it all and found my 'man conquering beast' foolishness the absurd tomfoolery that it must appear to other life forms.

I can't call this moment paradise found, I enter high places whenever fishing enters my mind. It's enough to describe it as a very high point in a remarkable adventure. I released twenty four brown trout that day, about half by intention. And so, with varying numbers, the delicious days went by, long hours of fishing, thinking about fishing and tasty evening teas and conversation—almost always about fishing. Immersed in an element I covet like wolves crave the company of their fellow hunters there were even hard-grabbing brown trout in my dreams.

Then came a melding of another of my deepest passions with angling—backpacking. Though I become more a home toting tortoise than a prowling predator, minimal fishing tackle at least keeps my hand in and now and then spares me one more freeze dried dinner. "Walk about" in Australian, a long dreamed of week-long solo trek through the outback of the Snowy Mountains found me, map in hand, backpacking through the high country of Kosioski National Park. Here are millions of undisturbed acres sparsely intersected by streams and rivers. Though hot, almost arid in February, one passes ample water for drinking, cooking, an occasional refreshing dip and excellent mountain stream fishing. For one full week there was only one fast passing group of horsemen in search of "brumbys", wild horses and a young couple hiking from the direction I was headed. All the rest was solitude. Well not completely.

Like another time in Alaska when I was indulging my periodic yen for solitude, I remember waking one morning with the strangest feeling of being watched. My tent was on a remote beach in a hidden cove of Resurrection Bay, miles out from the quaint seacoast village of Seward and except for hundreds of sea birds, foxes, rabbits, black bears and the big bluetick hound sleeping beside me, isolation was mine. I suppose in the end it's only separation from my own kind that draws me to unpeopled environs. The question is whether it's disenchantment with humanity or a disturbing self reflection I see in others that precipitates my escapes.

Anyway I woke up slowly, uneasy somehow, almost dreading to look out of the tent to the misty water. Pushing away sleepy images of hungry bears I raised up and faced the feeling. There were six large seals, just their heads out of the becalmed water, soundless, dead still and with huge unblinking eyes staring at me as intently as Miss Bonnet my eighth grade algebra teacher used to do while waiting for my excuse for not having done my homework. They suffered my return stare for just an instant then vanished like a switched off flashlight beam.

The point is that even on either of the polar caps there is no 'alone' and how arrogant we are to think so. I learned it several more times in the Snowies. During a moonlit night for one, I

heard sounds like someone trying to tear down an old tin cattleman's shack near where I was camped. It turned out to be that droll mix of small bear and large woodchuck, doubtless marsupial, called a wombat. He peered at me for a moment, saw me holding my ground and went back to his noisy midnight task I felt certain with a grin.

Every morning with the cool approach of dark, shadows solidified into moving creatures rabbits, foxes and kangaroos in various sizes. It was all quite magic. Then on the next to my last night there, I camped on a sort of mesa overlooking a huge long valley. It was after eleven, me asleep with the pleasant exhaustion of long hours walking in the sun, when a light flashing over the tent disturbed me. At first I thought it was a dream but now aroused it passed over again. Was it a late hiker, just arriving, and using a light to pitch his tent? It happened again.

When I went outside to see who was there it turned out to be a massive thunder storm too far up the valley to hear the thunder. Lightning had illumined my tent. I went back to the coziness of my sleeping bag and began to snooze. The next thing that woke me was the growing loudness of rolling thunder as the tempest moved closer and closer. Then crashing, earsplitting, lightning bolts were bombarding the ground around me and I knew how ants must feel when a troop of Marines marches over their ant hill. I thought that if it happens here in this way there won't be a speck left of me. I'm pretty sure I trembled.

The storm passed, I was overwhelmed with relief and fell back into a deep dreamless slumber. But after awhile I began seeing the lights again, a nightmare perhaps? No, it was another storm as intense as the first and coming from the same direction. It too passed over me and I remembered the saying that lightning never strikes twice in the same place. Having escaped once I wished that it would. It didn't get me the second time either and believe it or not, just before dawn, a third storm followed the second. It was like my first marriage, terrifying yet wonderful and in the end I escaped.

I walked for long, hot, dry miles the last day. I wanted to camp near my pick up point by evening as I had promised Mike I'd appear there by mid morning. There was water from a small creek near lunch time but none during the afternoon and a blazing sun caused me to soon exhaust my canteen. When at last I came around the side of the high hill and spotted the sparkling blue river below me I went down to it like baby ducks go to mill ponds.

Fast out of shirt and shorts I can't describe the cooling exhilaration that swept over me in the first instant of my plunge. I swam and floated around like some pampered potentate in his private pool for a long time and finally came out to lie on my inflatable sleeping pad beside my oasis. In moments I dozed off.

I don't like to kill fish and seldom do but I was into my sixth day of freeze dried noodles, starved for something, almost anything else and had been fantasizing all day about a fried trout. Asleep it was already browning crisply in my dream, the odor so tantalizing my mouth watered and my stomach longed for its nourishing warmth. If there was a taking fish in my swimming pool it was doomed.

I awoke just as evening began. The sun had gone down behind a hill and a chilly breeze touched my naked body. Shivering a bit I dressed and looked down the pool. Sure enough there were rises, two or three different ones and a little farther than the rest, a big one.

"That's dinner!" I whispered.

I don't know if I trembled from excitement about the possible size of the fish, the anticipation of high cuisine for dinner or still shivered from the sudden freshness but I almost dropped the pack rod assembling it. The fly was a bedraggled looking thing that several fish back had been a proud Royal Wulff. The big rise came again and I reached hard to cover it. It was a long cast, perhaps seventy feet, but with a helpful breeze it appeared it would make it. Yet just as it was over its mark I jerked back in disbelief. From the center of the expanding rings popped up a head, a miniature of my almost forgotten Alaskan seals. A creature that not even many Australians have seen in the wild, it was a duck-billed platypus. We exchanged surprised stares and it undulated, otter like, back under. Amazing!

The aborted fly meanwhile landed a few feet away, was gulped by a fat fourteen inch brown trout at the instant it hit and I, though dumbfounded, managed to bring the fish to hand. Kookaburras from somewhere up the now dark hill laughed and laughed as I gently, very gently released my fish fry. After such an incredible series of events there didn't seem to be anything further my predator nature could ask of this superb and wondrous place.

"O, the gallant fisher's life,
It is the best of any;
'T is full of pleasure, void of strife,
And't is beloved by many;"

—Izaak Walton, 1653. ▓

Mike Spry teaching a class.

FACING PAGE: Tumut River, Snowy Mountains.

7
NOVEMBER SPRING

They arrived in the spring of November to "free the people", roving, armed predators, above the law. They came on the vast Ibanez sheep ranch, ran off the family that had settled and built up the place for three generations and gave it all to the down-trodden thereabouts. Most were the ranch's employees. By late fall the hacienda lay in ruins, what sheep hadn't been eaten at endless fiestas or killed by pumas and foxes had run off and the free people faced the long Patagonian winter with nothing.

After four hours driving a primitive gravel highway from the small Chilean coastal town of Chaiten through awesome southern Andean scenery we stopped the aged Carryall at the top of a long hill. Having seen mammoth glaciers, thousands of blossoming red notros and soft pink roses, the road winding through lush green primal forests filled with giant coyhue trees, adult before we were born, what more marvels could the day offer? Yet I was struck dumb by the vista before us.

It was my first look at the enchanted Valley of Espolon. On that November afternoon, sunshine glowing over snow-capped mountains from nearby Argentina backlit a setting lovelier than fifty years of outdoor adventure had prepared me. Cascading out and down from a steep, granite ravine to the left tumbled the entire flow of the turquoise tinted Rio Espolon. It meanders then through opulent grassy meadows and rolling cattle and sheep pastures bordered by tall greenleafed Lombardi poplars.

This classic little river is a provocative series of long shallow riffles filling deep, dark, almost still pools before vanishing around high ground to the right for its eventual confluence with grander Rio Futaleufu. An uncommon medley of aesthetics like these could well explain why God was further inspired to create that most divine creature—the trout. Yet I was aroused too by another emotion.

In deja-vu fashion I felt a strange familiarity, as though this was somehow home. Yet if it was some final destination, the ultimate environs discovered, wow, what a journey to get here!

It began in the forties in the gentler climes of eastern Virginia, another world where spring comes In April. A skinny boy beside a tiny pool, on a tiny stream, a twenty minute bike ride from his house. A certain mayfly floating into view of my dog and I one afternoon as we delved the deeps with a hook impaled earthworm, a spark ignited.

Though until that moment overlooking Espolon I had never thought of fishing as the vehicle for a half century quest for permanency, this same passion had led me as far east as the magic isles of Nippon, south to the Snowy Mountains of Australia, north for twenty years in Alaska, to almost every area of Canada and the United States known for angling. And now deep into the Chilean Andes. So why was this? This unexpected homecoming? Yet other questions remain.

After two decades in Alaska why would anyone whose principal activity is fly fishing decide to leave that Mecca of Meccas? Had the last of the best freshwater fishing in the world changed? Was it no longer as good? Had it become too crowded, no more a vast pristine wilderness offering unmatched aesthetics? Or was a lifelong boy at last growing mellow, less intrigued with wild environs, encounters with angry bears, the stimulation of risky white water? Could the time have come, at last, when a pastoral scene was more satisfying than to gaze over trackless tundra, sheep and cattle grazing green pastures more comforting than watching a wolf pack stalk a caribou? Or was it something else? I am still not sure but the pull was too strong to deny. We camped beside the river that night.

I woke the next morning before the others and went to the river. Long light of early dawn caused dew drops on wild rose blossoms to twinkle more fetchingly than tinsel tree ornaments. As the sun topped a nearby ridge it was a curtain going up on a well-lit stage. A hundred birds from trees and bushes I didn't know began singing songs I had never heard. I saw some. Quetelhues, a species of lapwing, like Arctic terns though a bit larger dove at me, scolding in a raucous tone. Bandurias, ibis, large, long-beaked, prehistoric, flew high in loose formation, wing movements slow, clacking in their peculiar dialect. Every sight and sound as delicious and new to me as the first magic time I heard chamber music.

I recalled my first backpack camp in Alaska. Laying awake in my sleeping bag, listening, it struck me that for the first time in my adult life, after years of sleeping out in eastern states, I didn't recognize a single Alaskan wild sound. In Virginia, bird, critter or insect, if it made a noise I knew what it was, where it was and what it was doing. I hadn't thought about it until then. Twenty years later I had grown as at home in those northern environs as in any other but here—once again—everything was new.

My best angling efforts produced two tiny rainbows, eager and gallant though not what we had come to find. Still I was euphoric over the surroundings and the exhilaration of discovery when I heard my pals getting up and returned to help with packing. We had decided the night before to breakfast in the village of Futaleufu as the map showed it only a few kilometers further. Then, with the last of the gear stowed for the day's travel Marcelo Contreras, a Chilean companion, took an ancient spinning outfit missing two rod guides and cast a rusted spoon into the pool beside the vehicle. It was a short cast, almost to the end of what line was on the reel.

He didn't appear surprised when a five pound brown trout snatched his lure nor was his short line any disadvantage. Thirty pound monofilament, if a bit frayed here and there was still more than a match for the fish, the flimsy rod, bent to perilous strain, in more jeopardy than anything. It was a bit traumatic though when we insisted on releasing the trout. But Marcelo had already detected enough madness in his gringo amigos to handle it with suffering patience.

Futaleufu was picturesque and quaint, the people friendly and helpful. It's little more than an hour's drive from the fabled fishing grounds around Argentina's Esquel. But we had come on a specific mission. I was here, now a year later, at the behest of the Puyuhuapi Lodge for a three month survey of surrounding fishing. With Marcelo and a stateside guide we were to explore much larger Rio Futaleufu. The lodge owners hoped to expand their offerings.

A mountain view of the village of Futaleufu, Chile.
FACING PAGE: Jim Butler on the lower portion of the Futaleufu.

Jim Repine with Futaleufu River rainbow.
Kevin Kennedy photo

We were almost to the border before pulling into a farm and asking for permission to camp and fish for a day or two. Fate or whatever, our choice was a winner. We pitched tents under two huge, spreading (I didn't know what kind then) coyhue trees with a wide view of the river and surrounded by a grand profusion of blossoming wild rose bushes, hundreds of them, some taller than our heads. We began rigging up. Yet how do you prepare for a river you know nothing of? How do you choose rod sizes, line configurations or fly patterns when you have so little information?

The rumors we had come on made vague reference to "truchas grandes" (large trout), nothing more. Rainbows? Browns? Both? I began with a six weight, eight and a half foot rod and a balanced line with a ten foot sinking tip. It's a fair exploratory combination with a number eight Black Woolly Bugger. But this was southern Chile and that means Pancora Crabs, right? Well, nothing in fishing, gracias a Dios, is absolute.

The Pancora, typical to so much of the Patagonian fresh water fishery, is a dark, funny little thumb-sized half crab, half crawfish critter that moves with the same, 'stuck in reverse', spurting motion of its cousins. And while I have seen one or two attempts at simulated patterns, Black or Purple Woolly Buggers or leeches, given comparable action near or on the bottom, seem to emulate things well enough to excite crab-feeding trout. Anyway the leech worked though for none of the well-theorized reasons above.

I have since learned that pancoras don't inhabit this portion of the watershed, but trout on all four continents where I have pursued them can often be enticed to grab dark things that wiggle. It is the same on the Futaleufu. Yet it was not an Alaskan type 'fish-a-cast' bonanza. In fact, for me, it was more satisfying.

There were no more than a dozen fish during a long afternoon, an equal mix of rainbows and browns with nothing over eighteen inches, but as I moved slowly from one likely looking situation to another this big river (called Rio Grande in Argentina), more and more revealed reassuring normalcy. Though not easy the fish were where they should have been and behaving as good trout do.

If one read the water well and cast with a skillfully mended presentation the odds were not bad. That has become a much more gratifying situation for me these days than water jammed with instant takers.

Though in love with the river when I left, at first it didn't seem like prolific enough angling to satiate the typical 'Norte Americano' who has come from an opposite season of plentiful salmon runs, and salmon size trout. The 'trucha grande' tales had not proven out. Trying to weigh things in my mind during coffee and a sandwich the questions the lodge owner would need answered at least began to clarify.

What does it take to satisfy an angler who has traveled many expensive miles to enjoy one or two priceless weeks? What are most people really seeking? Is southern Chile the Alaska or Montana opposite season counterpart? And will this fragile, still unspoiled land gain or lose from an influx of visiting fly fishers?

The first answer isn't difficult. It's just a matter of honest, accurate presentation of expectations. A brochure, letter or magazine article that describes big fish in impressive numbers attracts anglers who are interested in big fish in impressive numbers. Simple! Nor is it to say there are not some days, in some places here, when and where you can have this level of sport. But to come away from Chile feeling fulfilled and happy big fish in impressive numbers shouldn't be the thing you hang your hopes on.

As to the second question, is Chile like other famous fisheries? I remember other times in other places. Like the Australian outback. There are no platypuses here to fool me. Nor will I share water in Chile with mega brown bears as in Alaska, or hear the flute-like sounds of mountain pigeons along the 'Iwana' (mountain char) streams that drain the misty ridges of northern Honshu. These unique delights, and innumerable others, are parts of their own special places.

Happily, Chile is Chile. Needful of no comparisons, this superb compilation of geography offers excellent trout populations, rainbow, brook and brown trout, in a wide variety of rivers, streams and lakes. Beginning a hundred miles or so north of Santiago, in semi desert country shaded with tall cactus, and extending south for two thousand miles through every type of eco-clime to the southern tip of Tierra Del Fuego, excellent trout populations abound.

While it is true that the noted Lake District, a two hundred and fifty mile scenic wonderland between Temuco and Puerto Montt has in some cases suffered overkill, there is still fine fishing there. The farther south one goes after that, the less exploited fishing will be, and Tierra Del Fuego though barren and wind swept, is the unquestioned least 'hit on', fish-filled wilderness left on the planet.

The majestic Andes loom high over the Lake District including some of earth's most beautiful, snow-coned volcanoes. There are less aggravating insects in Chile than I encounter in the other places mentioned, no poisonous snakes or any dangerous critters for that matter. And best of all are the people. They are friendly, if a bit reserved at first meeting, they like visitors and there are not many of them. Fourteen million inhabitants with almost half living in or around Santiago leaves rural Chile refreshingly uncrowded.

Now, as lovely as all I have written to this point must seem, there remains the question of how will an invasion of foreign anglers impact these marvelous surroundings? There is no doubt that nothing would be worse. Anything even approaching the maddening crowds in Montana or Alaska would, in only two or three seasons, destroy all of what is here. I cannot emphasize enough how fragile these trout populations are. Water systems here don't have anything like the insect populations of the western United States. Nor do millions of spawning salmon feed Chile's trout with roe, smolt and carcasses as in Alaska.

Combined with the nightmarish fact that Chile's government is environmentally asleep, that most Chileans in lamentable ignorance kill every fish they catch and that regulations are outdated and rarely enforced, it's easy to see that any degree of additional pressure would be negative. Please, unless you come here as not only a strong conservationist, but also a bearer of the conservationist word, understand that you will only be contributing to the destruction of one of the last superb angling areas left. Large trout in Chile are old trout.

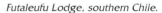

Futaleufu Lodge, southern Chile.

I returned to the water about a half hour before sunset. In the minute or two it took to wade out to a riffle edge, where the right cast would drift the fly down bouncing shallow water and onto a slick over a sharp drop off, it became apparent that something was different. What was it?

Picking my way with caution, trying to concentrate on just where to place each step in the diminished visibility of evening, my mind (never so sharp) wasn't bringing this new element to definition. It was only some vague blinking in my cerebral electronics. Then it flashed. Those little 'things' bumping into my face were—guess what? Insects! Bugs! Flies! Eureka!

"This is fly fishing and those are—flies." I grinned witlessly in the dim light as I mumbled.

Equipment readjusted to floating line, wispy leader and a size sixteen Royal Wulff, the first cast went out. I had moved downstream a bit to give the Wulff a longer drift over the slick. About mid way along its pilgrimage there was a deep, thick swirling, rise—but a good two feet farther down current than my fly. There was also that shock you receive sometimes when you are attuned to one size fish and something much larger appears. My blood began to heat.

On the next cast I put the fly too far into the white water. It drowned before reaching the slick. I false cast several times, drying hackles and calming nerves. The next cast went well. As satisfied with it as I was, a long, thick bodied 'truchas grande' grabbed the Wulff, about faced, and raced off down the Futaleufu.

I get goofy now and then, doubtless in preview of fast approaching senility, and in the short time it took for this bulldoggish, old brown to reach the end of his first run, my mind flashed through a vivid series of treasured images:

A big spray-showering Talachulitna River rainbow trout, appeared frozen high in the air against a glowing background of brilliant yellow, sunlit cottonwood leaves. Next a mist-shrouded first dawn on the Grande Cascapedia, Atlantic salmon fishing in marvel-filled eastern Canada faded quickly into an unforgettable afternoon on Montana's Bitterroot River when a very slow day ignited, as if by sorcery, into twenty minutes of action-filled bedlam.

Back a half century in wide-eyed astonishment I saw a gigantic largemouth bass explode in slow motion up, up, up and, at last, out of the glassy surface of Lakeside Lake in Virginia. As he shook his huge head my Jitterbug hanging from just inside his gaping mouth, he seemed so large that I feared what he might do to me for sticking him. I was ten and skinny, the bass was fat though not more than three pounds.

My present fish jolted my reveries. He sulked for a moment before doing a splashy surface roll and then sped off to the left under a large, brushy submerged log. If there is sanctuary at hand, depend on a smart old brown to find it.

From what I could see of the roll and feel of the fish's pull, he was over ten pounds. And from what I know now of the Futaleufu this is possible. As I stood in the water, the light almost gone, and examined the broken leader one last reflection came to me.

Most of my other favorite haunts were either frozen and snow-bound as in Alaska or at best not the warm inviting adventures they would become again in May. Here, after a day in short sleeves, I had on a light sweater only because of a slight evening chill.

Walking slow out of the river towards the campfire of my amigos I felt happy and somehow 'at home' with thoughts that this was not so much the end of an evening as it was the beginning of a season. Warmer and warmer days were ahead, many of them. And whether or not my long journey was over, a world of new adventures lay ahead. It was spring after all, the spring of November.

> "Oh Sir, doubt not but that Angling is an art; is it not an art to deceive a Trout with an artificial fly—a Trout!"
>
> —Izaak Walton, 1653. ✳

Special Note:

You may find it interesting to know about the two men from the Unites States who started the Alaskan-style, float plane lodge even farther south than Futaleufu near the town of Puyuhuapi. After my marvelous week there it seemed to me the place would flourish, but it was not to be.

I didn't know then that the weather we enjoyed was far from typical for the southern coast. Later there were too many days when flying raged from miserable to terrifying to impossible. Different than traveling by float plane in Alaska, challenging enough on its own, the mountain passes here are much more narrow, often offering no turn around options. Wind conditions are the most varietal I have ever flown through, accurate weather predictions hopeless and there are no pilot reports. This more than anything caused the lodge to fail. Yet with a few days of reasonable visibility and fair winds, it would be hard to imagine a more pleasant fishing week.

Futaleufu at dawn.

FACING PAGE: Chris Clarke with guide Kevin Kennedy, Futaleufu River.

FOUR MAGIC EVENINGS IN MARCH

For a hundred and fifty years the magnificent Chilean coyhue had survived disease and storm to grow to amazing height and girth. Three large men would have had to stretch hard to join arms around its scaly trunk. The coyhue had lived through the world's greatest wars, plagues, famines, social, political and industrial revolutions—old before the first airplane flew. Hidden deep in an ancient primal forest in quiet company with its kin, for all those years it sheltered and sustained countless creatures large and small. But greed-crazed predators found the coyhue. Mindless men with chain saws brought it crashing to its death in minutes.

Giant coyhue tree.

I went to the river late. It was the first of March in Patagonia, the clients had left that morning. There would be no other lodge guests for a week which left Hatchi, my dog, and I free to fancy pre fall marvels in solitude. I had no idea what was to come.

We were four nights away from a full moon, enjoying warm days of near cloudless sunshine and while I have never leaned toward lunar phases effecting fishing, my wife isn't convinced.

"Are you sure?" She smiles when I try to debunk such things. But then she is Chilean, sometimes signing notes and letters to me:

"Tu brujita" It means "Your little witch."

In any event at Second Run, a place on our hideaway portion of the Futaleufu River that competes hard as my all-time favorite fishing hole, almost nothing was happening at seven p.m. As I sat on the log bench we have beside the water, there was a half-hearted rise now and then, fish taking caddis emergers, catchable by nymphing but I had come with 'dry flies upstream only,' in mind. Hatchi, a hundred pound (at nine months) Japanese Akita with a disposition like the roly poly bear cub he resembles, was content stalking and trying to pounce on various grasshoppers.

Old traditions can be stodgy, impeding effectiveness yet there is virtue too often forgotten in establishing rules of sportsmanship, setting parameters that even the odds a little between players. Like the agreeable feeling of winning at any game, doing it cleanly within defined rules enhances satisfaction. I don't always fish this way but once in awhile it puts one in touch with other customs on other beats.

Since 7:30 p.m. is the usual time for cocktails at our lodge it had been a long time since I had been on the river at this hour. The evening glow, soft breeze and pleasure of time spent with a good friend made just sitting and thinking more attractive than the angling odds of the moment. Angling with a fly is called fishing's contemplative form.

Sonia and I bought a small farm in a very remote valley on the river sometime back and converted the house into a little fishing lodge. It's fly fishing, catch and release only, and accommodates only four guests. Adventure with this madness, high, low sad and hilarious, I'll save for another book but in more than fifty years on the water it's the first time I have lived beside a river and it's added a dimension to my angling I hadn't known. Now when I go to the water, it's to familiar, 'home places'; First and Second Runs, the Drop Off Hole, The Island with Jimito's Corner or The Other Side with The Rock Point Drift.

I can name other spots, the Talachulitna River in Alaska or Moose Creek in the Bitterroot Selway/Wilderness for example, that I have been on repeatedly and loved for a long time but my relationship with them was never as intimate as here. Dating a girl is nothing like living with her.

Rivers and streams have varied moods. Not human things they are myraid river and stream things caused by vagaries of weather, shifting water flow, changing environmental surroundings, critters, from birds and insects to mammals, reptiles and fish, around, on, and in their water and with ever-accelerating frequency, destruction caused by the abusive activities of guess who?—us! Water's cosmetics are light and shade, its voice infinite tonal levels, gurgling, splashing, murmuring and roaring. Again, like your favorite lady, you may get to know it better than anyone else, yet you won't learn it all from any river or stream in a single lifetime.

Second Run is a hundred yard long, fine gravel bar covered by a fairly brisk water flow. It extends out about eighty feet, the water deepening to the dark blue of a drop off. I think I've learned that in general brown trout inhabit the recesses of the gravel and rainbows hang around the blue edge. Though on any day you depend on this the opposite will be true. All summer there is a good morning hatch of light tan caddis in about a size sixteen and from December on mixed with lovely brown mayflies. During the height of the hatch, about an hour after sunlight reaches the water, both species of trout gath-

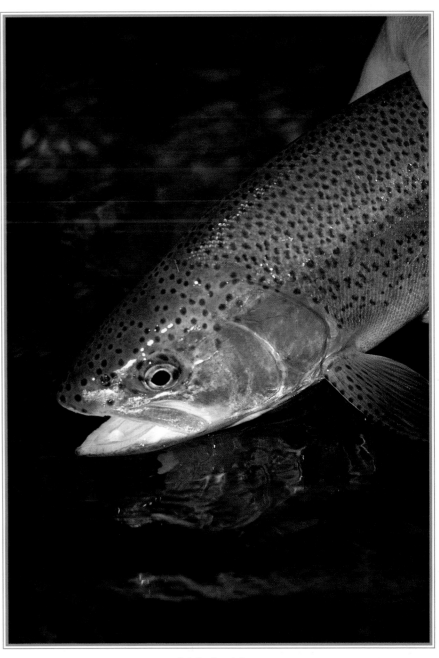

Futaleufu rainbow.
FACING PAGE: Master angler Lee Wulff.

My favored Futaleufu rod.

er over the flat and feed with greedy abandon. Given their sparse numbers during the rest of the day, it's amazing to see so many hungry fish make their sudden appearance.

They aren't large by some anglers standards, twelve to sixteen inches, but with four weight rods, etc., it's a half hour of incredible action. And Futaleufu's trout are the most energetic fighters I (and everyone who comes here) have encountered. More than once I've been running, deep into backing, convinced the fish I had on was at least five pounds and then have it turn out to be a fat, silvery two pounder. As I pondered important things like moods, feminine and aquatic, what nymph in my collection might come closest to the emergers still inspiring what few rises there were, things changed.

My reveries lasted through 7:30, the sun gone down beyond the tree-topped hills across the river. Falling temperature chilled the breeze. I slipped a rain jacket over my shirt, windbreaker enough for then, and I noted a rise out near the drop off. It was different, more aggressive perhaps or made by a larger fish. I watched for another. None came. The mesmerizing effect of passing water lulled me by its rhythmic flow. Hectic confusion that passes through most of our waking hours stilled, my thoughts seemed to crystallize.

Yes, I'm a predator, that's why I'm sitting here now, waiting for trout to behave in a particular way. It may be why dogs, such unaplogetic adherents to the same persuasion, have always been my best friends. Predation satisfies me. Not exactly true! The satisfaction is at best temporary. Can satisfaction be temporary! Semantics! Who cares? What I do when I fish is an integral part of my nature and when I don't do it for any length of time my spirit begins to wither. "My God! You could have fished today!", something inside me chides on almost any day that I don't. Yet if those predators I feel closest to, beasts, birds, insects and fish, weren't hungry would they still need to hunt. Hatchi's well-fed stomach offered no rest to the hoppers. I don't know! I do!

The next impressive rise came just minutes before eight. I heard it and looked up in time to see a fourteen incher in mid air. In lowering light it appeared to be a rainbow. I brushed a breeze-blown caddis off my face, then another blew into the back of my neck. It was the beginning of an insect blizzard but these weren't the morning bugs that had been around all season. They were larger, twelves or fourteens, and darker, more brown. As though someone turned on a switch, fish began rising all over the run, sometimes a dozen or more at once.

Most anglers experience these kinds of hatches now and then but I'm always amazed at where all the fish come from. Where were they until then? There must have been a hundred or more trout over the flat where no more than a dozen seemed to be all day. My excitement became instant fever, as I false cast and waded into position.

My number sixteen Elk Hair Caddis was gobbled as it hit the water.

"Dear Lord, look at it now!" I said to no one, as large mayflies began dancing in the air among the caddis.

Anxious to get my fish in and cast again I wished the tough, high-jumping rainbow was smaller, not so energetic. Greed in the land of plenty? Soon enough my over-eager pressure pulled the hook loose and I was ready to go for another. But the next drift produced nothing. Nor did the next or the one following. The problem was my fly was too small—I thought—and there was nothing else in my boxes that was similar, of any size. I changed to a number twelve Humpy but in failing light it took a while to tie it to the leader.

Something large grabbed the fly at the end of its first drift with enough force to snap the tippet. I was panicky but after much fumbling found the fly's clone and began trying to tie it on. It was a long, long struggle as I held fly and leader high in the air trying to silhouette them against the last light in the sky. Somehow I made it, at last, and was ready to fish. Poised to cast I looked down the run. Gorgeous moonlight replaced evening glow over the river, but I could see the water then was void of any activity. Nothing, not an insect in the air, no rises, or other sign that anything happened there that evening. My overgrown puppy sat watching, head cocked to one side. I could swear he was smiling, but I hadn't seen him catch a damned grasshopper either!

The next evening I came to the water prepared. A couple of hours at the tying table had produced a half dozen ultimate patterns, Elk Hair Caddis's, larger, darker, closer to the color of the naturals. It was seven o'clock again, an hour to wait if action was to repeat on schedule, but an hour on the bench beside Second Run can slip by before your second or third contemplation resolves.

Bandurias, out of sight upriver, were clacking in profusion as various bands gathered into their high roost trees. Huge old coyhues where these curious birds spend their nights, have hosteled such clients for countless ages. They loom high over the river across from Jimito's Corner and many evenings the nightly conclave's clamor heralds the start of amazing rainbow

FACING PAGE: Trout shadow under water.

action. All over southern Chile though the giant old trees are being destroyed for the greedy, quick bucks they bring as wood chips. From Puerto Montt, mountains of these chips are being shipped to Japan to be made into newsprint—and toilet paper. God forgive us such atrocities!

At seven thirty the wind picked up, perhaps enough to keep flying insects off the water. I felt a stab of doubt. It might be that my hour of quiet thought was wasted. Whoa! What kind of goofy idea is that? Why did Walton put so much store in just that aspect of angling? *The Compleat Angler* Is subtitled, *The Contemplative Man's Recreation*.

To sit for a while, to become still, to breathe and think in rhythm and at peace with such comely surroundings; where is there more therapeutic treatment for mind, body or soul? Yet it's my predatory nature that brings me here. It's been that baser impulse in fact, more than opportunity for poetic meditation, that has caused me to go to unspoiled places and linger in them. If I hadn't been so intrigued with the capture of wild creatures I may never have discovered the higher joy of freeing them. Or given the myriad of my other weaknesses my predatory urges might have been perverted toward far worse endeavors.

At eight o'clock the wind stilled as if by holy command, moonlight out-glowed the sun's last glimmers and bugs rained down while my meticulously replicated elk hair phonies floated through, beside and around a hundred or more swirls and rises—untouched. The most eager takes this time were going to a large, number six size bug that best resembled a bushy mosquito. I took one fish on a like-sized Humpy seconds before the action turned off. Hatchi bounced through silver shadows along the trail home with more animated spirit than me.

The hatch began at seven fourty-five on the third evening. Was it early for some peculiar reason or was my watch slow, as at times it's prone to be? I still don't know but my bushy number six mosquito was a flop, its inspiration from the night before failing to appear. It was like sticking a bloody finger into a swarm of piranhas and still not getting a bite. At the last minute of the rise I managed to hook a couple of fish with a store-bought size fourteen Elk Hair Caddis, but that's not the same. Animal behaviorists warn us not to attribute human qualities to what we observe in dogs but I was sure from the way he didn't want to walk home close to my side,

Angler Darren Bell on second run.

Hatchi was embarrassed to be associated with such an oafish predatorial role model.

Then came the evening of the full moon. With all the magic connected with this phenomenon, plus my three previous educating evenings, I went to the river with trepidation. The wind at seven thirty was the highest yet, no question enough to blow away the hatch but the huge moon was already up over the mountains. I sat mesmerized as every object in sight transformed from deepening orange to radiant platinum. No man-made light show ever rivaled this exquisite spectacle. Hatchi seemed as affected as me. Even in the most unspoiled environs happenings this stirring are rare.

At eight o'clock once again the wind dropped to a slight breeze, the air filled with insects and fish went wild. And the pattern I had worked out that morning, a number twelve sort of half caddis, half mayfly was hot. Every time I played by English chalk stream rules and cast upstream—boomba—fish on! Mid way through the long, reel screaming run of my third fish, Hatchi sat down beside the river, raised his muzzle to the moon and sang as haunting and as wild a howl as any Sioux warrior's death wail or timber wolf's spine-chilling prayer to the hunt. I will carry this image to my grave.

Yet all of my lessons haven't come from raccoons, dogs and rainbow trout or through long streamside meditation. There has been a rare man here and there with as much to teach. Bill Negley was one.

"It happened in Africa. I had just shot an arrow deep into the chest of a huge male lion," Bill spoke with a Texas accent. Not the course rasping twang popularized in country music but a soft, patrician dialect once heard from "well-born" folks from Virginia south. "That done, as you may know, one must retreat quickly so the animal doesn't feel pressed and compelled to attack. But our 'hunter', a Portuguese fellow who surely did know lions but not bow hunting, elected to stand fast. 'Shoot him again!' He kept saying! It was a mistake."

Baseball great Ted Williams looking at silver salmon in Alaska.

As the old gentleman related the story he raised his arm bringing a ten weight, ten foot graphite rod up with it. Thirty feet of line sailed out behind him and went through a faultless looping movement. At the correct instant the long rod bent forward, shooting the airborne line thirty feet and another thirty of loose line laying coiled in the water beside him, in a long accurate cast.

The fly, a home-tied pattern looking something like a comet, polar shrimp cross with an orange Mylar body and white polar bear wing, landed some twenty feet upcurrent from where we had just seen a heavy boil. It was sure to reach a swing around on its downriver drift, within inches of where the salmon should be holding. We watched the fluorescent yellow running line moving with the current.

"We had been tracking this old male for three days and had on one occasion come to a point where he had circled and secretly looked us over as we followed the trackers. There was no doubt he knew he was being harassed. And in fact who was doing it." Bill's attention was

Sonia Repine.

Trout sign Futaleufu Lodge.

directed to the drifting fly as it swung, hopefully, in front of an agitated chum salmon, fresh from the Bering Sea. They were bright silver and out to do battle with anything getting in the way of their just begun spawning runs. The Comet Shrimp stopped its swing. The fisherman gave it a tantalizing swimming motion by twitching the rod tip. Nothing happened.

"The problem is, an arrow takes awhile to kill, no matter how well placed. If you leave quickly the animal will normally lay down and die. But here we were facing a wounded lion that had been getting angrier each day for three days. And since I had stood up in the vehicle to shoot, he even knew which one of us had done the deed."

Bill had pursued his bow hunting passion until he then claimed more dangerous game killed than any archer living or dead. I was fishing with him on the Unalakleet River in northwest Alaska and it was obvious his angling skills were a match for his archery prowess.

The Unalakleet is sixty miles of long runs, cut banks and occasional deep holes. It drains westward through rolling tundra hills about a hundred and eighty miles south of Nome, emptying into the Bering Sea. Pacific salmon, kings, chum, pinks and silvers run the river in sometimes unbelievable numbers. Char are thick and can exceed ten pounds and Arctic grayling fishing is superb. Dry fly anglers can expect fifty fish grayling days, at times with several of these huge-finned beauties in trophy class.

We were fishing for chum, the rarest species of sport-caught salmon in the Northwest, fly fishing for these tough game fish that can go over twenty pounds is one of Alaska's best kept secrets. Bill's second cast was ten feet or farther downriver but his line maintained the same drifting configuration.

"The hunter jumped out of the vehicle, scrambling for his rifle, the movie photographer, grinding away but prepared to run. I was crouched down in the open Land Rover, arms over my head for protection, the lion in full charge, coming for me. I remember the great beast smashing into the truck and feeling sharp claws grasping my arms."

"Whoa! There he is!"

The story was interrupted by a twelve pound, protein-charged chum that nailed the fly as it drifted to a momentary presentation inches off the bottom in front of the fish. All the energy built and stored over the last few months of frenzied feeding in preparation for the spawning journey was unleashed now in a reel-smoking downstream run. Bill was deep into his backing.

Excitement gleamed in the old predator's eyes as he deftly employed line give and take and an ever-steady rod pressure with the expertise of years. The feel of Iceland's Atlantic salmon, red fish from the Texas Gulf, Florida tarpon, Alaska's king salmon and countless other fish from streams, river and oceans all over the world came back. The throbbing life force transmitted from one creature to another via line and rod brings a deep, satisfying, impossible-to-explain sense of satisfaction to each of us who, now and then indulge our most natural, instinctive inclinations.

It was a long struggle but in time, with applied skill, even light leaders win out. Twenty minutes later Bill maneuvered the now tired salmon into a position near the opposite bank where I could slip the loop of my fish trailer around the base of its tail and pull up. The fish was suspended head down from the lasso. I handed it all to our guide who strained to hold it high enough for pictures. We were flushed with grins of success.

"And the bones in your hat are the 'floating bones' from that lion?" I queried Bill about his unusual decoration as we prepared to release the fish.

"Yes, Africans believe these bones, taken from the chest area, if carried with you will bring good luck." It seemed to work with salmon fishing.

"But how did you get away from the lion?" I remembered where the story had left off.

"Well the hunter at last got his rifle into play and happily, killed the lion and not me." Bill moved back into the stream. "But it greatly diminished the experience."

"In what way?" I asked.

He back cast only once before sending a tight looped sixty feet into the area where he felt other fish might be. As the drift began he turned his head just enough to assure his voice would reach me but never let his attention to the fly wander.

"My first reaction was a deep sense of gratitude at having come out of it alive. But then I was swept with a feeling of regret. My sorrow being that his magnificent creature had been killed by a foul."

The big rod bent again and a flashing explosion took place as the sea fresh salmon felt the hook. The fish took off downriver, Bill moving with him.

Over the next several days I got to know a gentle man, thoughtful and considerate of those around him, modest in the quiet, believable way sometimes seen in men of real accomplishment and a 'gentleman' in a near forgotten sense. It brought back thoughts and memo-

Jim and Sonia Repine with silver salmon on the Kenai River, Alaska. Jeff Moore photo

ries, images and feelings instilled in me years before by Ruark, Hemingway and others. It was the only time I met a man who killed a lion.

So there you have it, a long and varied look at my predator instinct, how it came about, was nurtured and matured—if it's your judgment that it has matured. My oldest friend from growing up years, a Pamunkey Indian from eastern Virginia, delights in assuring me that nothing has changed except my age, no more mellow than ever, I only get tired quicker. It could be. Yet here is one last thought.

Scripture maintains that God spoke through the prophet Isaiah some eight hundred and fifty years before Christ manifested in the flesh and said:

"All the wisdom of Man is foolishness to God.

Your thoughts are not my thoughts.

Your words are not my words."

Like the clause in a contract that explains all misunderstandings this might be the key to the unfathomable question of why a loving creator made us the most vicious, violent, warlike, hate-filled and destructive creatures ever to breathe air. Given our history and present social state, what sane argument could be made that our wisdom isn't at least foolish? Maybe, though this is why an instinct that appears dedicated to the destruction of others, an integral part of survival itself, can lead to the calming effects of meditation? Contained somewhere within ethical limits, the meditative practice of angling with a fly seems to have done so with me.

"I care not, I, to fish in seas
Fresh rivers best my mind do please
Whose sweet calm course I contemplate,
And seek in life to imitate."

—Izaak Walton, 1653. ▦

FOUR MAGIC EVENINGS IN MARCH

Mel Krieger

Jim Repine lives in Chile with his wife Sonia. They operate a trout fly fishing lodge in the southern part of Chile, high in the Andes Mountains. Jim Repine is the author of several books and spent many years in Alaska before falling in love with Chile. His angling and business experiences have taken him around the Pacific rim where he has enjoyed experiencing trout in many different beautiful and unusual settings.

Adolfo Nieto
04

LEARN MORE ABOUT FLY FISHING AND FLY TYING WITH THESE BOOKS

If you are unable to find the books shown below at your local book store
or fly shop you can order direct from the publisher below.

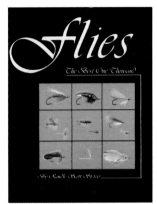

Flies: The Best One Thousand
Randy Stetzer
$24.95

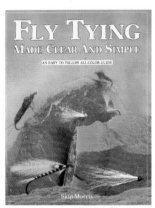

Fly Tying Made Clear and Simple
Skip Morris
$19.95 (HB: $29.95)

The Art of Tying the Dry Fly
Skip Morris
$29.95 (HB: $39.95)

Curtis Creek Manifesto
Sheridan Anderson
$7.95

American Fly Tying Manual
Dave Hughes
$9.95

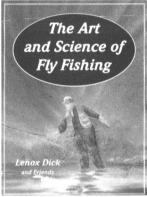

The Art and Science of Fly Fishing
Lenox Dick
$19.95

Western Hatches
Dave Hughes, Rick Hafele
$24.95

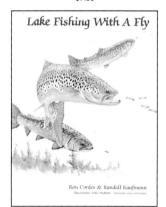

Lake Fishing with a Fly
Ron Cordes, Randall Kaufmann
$26.95

Advanced Fly Fishing for Steelhead
Deke Meyer
$24.95

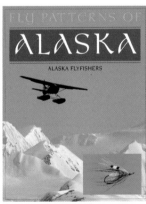

Fly Patterns of Alaska
Alaska Flyfishers
$19.95

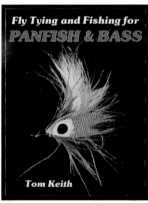

Fly Tying & Fishing for Panfish and Bass
Tom Keith
$19.95

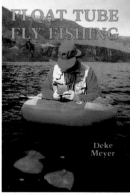

Float Tube Fly Fishing
Deke Meyer
$11.95

VISA, MASTERCARD or AMERICAN EXPRESS ORDERS CALL TOLL FREE: 1-800-541-9498
(9-5 Pacific Standard Time)

Or Send Check or money order to:

Frank Amato Publications
Box 82112
Portland, Oregon 97282

(Please add $3.00 for shipping and handling)